Trees: East

Steve Cafferty

Collins
An Imprint of HarperCollinsPublishers

ISBN: 978-0-06-089063-6
ISBN-10: 0-06-089063-0

FIRST EDITION

Text © Steve Cafferty 2007

Smithsonian Consultant: Stanwyn G. Shetler

HarperCollins books may be purchased for educational, business, or sales promotional use. For information in the United States, please write to: Special Markets Department, HarperCollins Publishers, 10 East 53rd Street, New York, NY 10022.

The name of the "Smithsonian," "Smithsonian Institution," and the sunburst logo are registered trademarks of the Smithsonian Institution.

Edited and designed by D & N Publishing, Berkshire, UK
Printed and bound by Printing Express Ltd, Hong Kong

10 09 08 07
9 8 7 6 5 4 3 2 1

PREFACE

Trees are so familiar and commonplace that we often take them for granted. It is usually only when great changes affect the tree population, such as the aftermath of major storms or the rapid loss of thousands of trees from disease, that we realize what a major element they are in the world around us. In fact, few people live in entirely treeless surroundings, even in towns and cities, and trees have an important influence on everyday living, whether directly or indirectly.

Trees perform a number of vital functions in the environment. Like all green plants, they are able to use the energy of sunlight to manufacture basic foods, such as sugars, on which all life depends. As part of this process, they also help maintain the level of oxygen in the atmosphere. Trees play a significant role in preventing the erosion of soil by binding it with their roots, and their dead leaves greatly improve soil fertility when they rot to form humus. They also provide habitats for other wildlife, both animals and other plants, that rely on trees for food and shelter. Humans have always relied heavily on trees, and many species have important commercial uses. As well as timber for fuel and building, they yield food and drink, forage for domestic stock, and a variety of other products ranging from cork, paper pulp, matches, dyes, and tanning agents to perfumes, medicines, gums, and even jewellery. Nowadays, there is a large industry based solely on the use of trees as ornamental and amenity plants to delight the eye and improve the quality of our own, man-made, habitat.

HOW TO USE THIS BOOK

This book covers 163 species of trees, including all those commonly found in the wild in the United States, as well as those frequently planted in streets and public parks and gardens.

Each page of the main section of the book has a **photograph** of a tree, and an illustration showing additional details. The common name of the tree is given, together with its scientific name, and the name of the plant family to which it belongs. At the top of each page is an indication of the tree's height, and whether it is evergreen or deciduous. The lighter portion of the **calendar bar** indicates those months in which you will usually find this tree in flower. For conifers, the lighter portion indicates when the tree is shedding pollen from male cones (where this information is not available the calendar bar has been omitted). This is meant only as a guide. Flowering can be brought forward or delayed by several weeks, depending on the seasonal weather conditions. It can also be affected by geography—as a general rule flowering is delayed for trees growing further north.

The **ID Fact File** lists features that will help you to identify each species, and the general text provides further information.

To identify a tree, look through the book to find the most likely match. Use the ID Fact File to see if the description matches the tree. If it does not, check any similar trees described on adjacent pages. The species are arranged in order of their closest relationships, so the tree you are trying to identify should be nearby.

HISTORY OF TREES IN THE US

Geologically speaking, the story of trees in the United States begins with the last ice age, which radically altered established populations and distributions. Many species would have retreated south with the advancing ice, or migrated to the slopes and ridges of high mountain ranges. Once the ice began to retreat northward, some species recolonized their original northern range. Others took the opportunity to expand their range or, in some cases, stayed in the warmer, more favorable conditions in the south. For all species in North America, however, this period defines current distributions (discounting human influence).

Several main forest types became established at that time: coniferous pine and birch forests generally developed in the north, with more broadleaf forest types emerging in the south. In the warmer conditions of the extreme south, evergreen forests became more common. Mountain slopes were covered with spruce and fir forests while lowland swampy areas were readily colonized by species of willow and alder. Oaks colonized the major mountain ranges in the east and on the central plains.

Sixteenth-century European explorers would have found great swathes of cedar, poplar, and oak forests in the east, and pines, spruces, and giant redwoods in the west. Some remarkable trees have adapted in ways specific to their local environment. Many western conifers, growing in arid areas prone to summer fires, are able to regenerate after exposure to flame. Others have developed ways of conserving water in desert habitats or have adapted to wet, swampy areas. Today, only fragments of these forests remain, and individual species have become endangered because of overexploitation and habitat loss.

Many species are today cultivated as well as being found in the wild; many others have been introduced and become naturalized. Both of these trends have an impact on wild populations. For trees cultivated since precolonial times, it is often difficult to ascertain the original native ranges since they were often moved around by people as they migrated across the plains cultivating useful plants. In other cases, introduced species may outcompete local, endemic species and thereby artificially change the makeup of local habitats. Nevertheless, fine examples of native American forest remain, many in the national parks.

WHAT IS A TREE?

Trees are woody plants which have a single, well-developed main stem or trunk which branches well above ground level, usually at a height of 6ft or more. The trunk and main branches are covered with a protective layer of bark. These are the only features which all trees have in common as trees do not belong to a single group of plants but are found in many different and unrelated plant families.

The division between shrubs and trees is rather blurred. Shrubs are also woody plants but are generally smaller, with several stems which branch at or near ground level. All of the species in this book will form trees where conditions are appropriate.

Unlike non-woody plants, trees grow in both height and girth each year. The increase in height is achieved simply by the elongation of the branches. The increase in girth is achieved by the addition of an extra layer of woody tissue on the trunk and branches. These layers can be seen as the annual rings exposed when a tree is felled.

Trees are often divided into evergreen and deciduous species. **Evergreens** shed and replace their leaves gradually over a period of years. The leaves are often leathery or waxy to reduce water loss or withstand the cold, so evergreens are typical of cold or mountainous regions, but are also common in hot, dry habitats. **Deciduous** trees shed all of their leaves each year, and remain bare through the winter. This allows the trees to remain dormant, husbanding their resources during the harshest season. Their leaves are generally thinner and more delicate than those of evergreens, and are more prone to wilting and frost damage.

Many trees reproduce by means of **flowers**, and the fruits and seeds which develop later. Those species which are wind pollinated often have tiny flowers, lacking sepals and petals; and the flowers appear well before the leaves in spring. Insect-pollinated trees have larger, more showy flowers, which are often produced later in the year. One large group of trees which does not have flowers is the conifers, so-called because of their cone-shaped reproductive organs.

GLOSSARY

Alternate With leaves scattered along the twig.
Anther Fertile tip of a stamen, containing pollen.
Bract Leaflike structure at base of leaf or cone scale.
Capsule Dry fruit usually splitting when ripe to release seeds.
Catkin Slender spike of tiny flowers usually lacking sepals and petals, and wind pollinated.
Cultivar Plant bred by gardeners, not occurring naturally in the wild.
Involucre Leaflike structure, usually green or greenish, surrounding flowers and fruits.
Leaflet Separate division of a leaf.
Native Originating from an area.
Naturalized Fully established in the wild in areas outside original distribution.
Opposite With leaves arranged in pairs along the twig.
Ovary Female part of a flower containing egg cells and, eventually, seeds.
Pinnate Divided into two rows of leaflets along a central axis.
Palmate Divided into leaves which spread from a single point like fingers of a hand.
Semi-evergreen Retaining most leaves in all except the harshest conditions.
Stamen Male part of a flower consisting of a slender stalk bearing the pollen sacks or anthers.
Stipule Small, leaflike structure at the base of the leaf-stalk.
Style Usually a slender organ on top of the ovary bearing a surface receptive to pollen.
Sucker New shoot growing from the roots of a tree.
Twice pinnate With each of the pinnate divisions themselves pinnately divided.
Trifoliolate With three leaflets.

IDENTIFYING TREES

All plants have specific characteristics, or combinations of characteristics, which enable them to be identified, even among species that have a similar overall appearance. Not all features are equally useful or even constant. Plants on rich soils, for example, tend to produce lush growth and may have larger leaves than plants of the same species growing on poor soils. Identifying trees can be more difficult than identifying herbaceous plants simply because the necessary parts are often out of reach and cannot be observed easily. However, with practice, identification can become quite easy. Always examine the tree and its parts closely and be sure you are comparing similar structures and not, for example, mistaking a stipule for a leaflet. The different parts of a tree and the characters they provide are described here as an initial guide to recognition.

The **height** of a tree varies considerably with age, soil depth, exposure, and other environmental factors. The heights given in this book are the maximum normally attained by each species; many individual trees will be smaller. The **crown** of the tree is made up of the branches and twigs. The outline or overall shape is often distinctive although it can vary with age. There may be a recognizable **pattern of branching** and the branches themselves may be arched or pendulous. Conifers often have branches in regular whorls which may clothe the trunk almost to the ground. Most non-coniferous trees have rather irregular branching patterns. **Twigs** can be hairy or colored. These characters generally occur only on young growth as hairs are lost with age, and older twigs become duller and darker. The presence or absence of spines on the twigs is also a useful distinguishing feature. The **trunk** provides few useful characters other than general features such as being short, stout or bare for most of its length.

Bark is less useful than is often supposed for identifying trees, but the overall color, texture, and whether the bark sheds in strips or flakes provide some clues. The texture varies with age to some extent, usually becoming rougher and often more cracked and fissured in old trees. Sometimes the outer layers of bark peel or flake to reveal brighter layers beneath.

Leaves are a major source of identification characters. Start by looking at their arrangement on the twigs: for example, are they alternate (scattered along the twig) or opposite? Are the leaves pinnately (with two rows of leaflets arranged along the central axis) or palmately divided (with leaflets spreading like fingers of a hand)? Are the leaves or leaflets lobed, toothed, or entire? All of these features are relatively constant and reliable. The size of the leaves is also important but spans a range rather than being a precise measurement as it can vary somewhat with age and growing conditions. Other useful features may include texture (whether thin or leathery), color (often different when unfolding in spring and frequently so in autumn), degree of hairiness, and the distribution of hairs on the leaf. Leaves are generally paler and more hairy on the underside than on their upper surface. **Stipules** are small, leaflike organs which occur at the base of the leaf-stalk in some species.

Flowers and **fruits** are also important. Look at the size and shape of the flowers. Are petals present and if so, how many are there and are they of equal size? The way in which the flowers are arranged is often a useful character, for example in spikes or clusters, or scattered singly along the twigs? Also note whether the flowers are borne on new wood, that is the current year's growth, or on old wood which is the lower, thicker parts of the twigs. Many trees have single-sexed flowers: male flowers have only stamens while female ones have an ovary and style but no stamens.

The type of fruit (fleshy, berry-like, dry), together with its size and color when ripe, also provides clues to identity. Only trees with hermaphrodite or female flowers bear fruit.

One group of trees, the **conifers**, bears cones instead of flowers and fruits. It includes firs, pines, and spruces. The pollen-bearing male cones are usually small and sometimes brightly colored. Female cones are larger, and the scales which make up the cone become woody as the seeds ripen. The shape and arrangement of the cone scales are important characteristics.

WHAT NEXT?

There are many opportunities to pursue your interest in native trees. Many organizations are dedicated to raising awareness of them, both at the national level and, especially, regionally. In addition, many arboretums and botanic gardens work for the conservation of native trees and other plants as listed below:

Alaska Botanical Garden (Anchorage, Alaska)
Arnold Arboretum (Jamaica Plain, Massachussets)
Chicago Botanical Garden (Glencoe, Illinois)
Marie Selby Botanical Garden (Sarasota, Florida)
Missouri Botanical Garden (St. Louis, Missouri)
New York Botanic Garden (New York, New York)
Rancho Santa Ana Botanic Garden (Claremont, California)

A wide variety of reference and popular books is dedicated to the trees of North America, or, trees in general:

The Encyclopedia of North American trees, by Sam Benvie. Richmond Hill, Ontario: Firefly Books, 2002.
The Firefly Encyclopedia of Trees, by Steve Cafferty (ed.). Richmond Hill, Ontario: Firefly Books, 2005.
Field Guide to North American Trees (2nd edition), by Thomas Elias. New York: Grolier, 1989.
The National Audubon Society Field Guide to North American Trees: Eastern Region, by Elbert Luther Little. New York: Knopf, 1980.
Flora of North America, by the Flora of North America Editorial Committee (eds.). New York: Oxford University Press, 2003.

Web Sites

Useful and informative Web sites include the following:

http://www.borealforest.org/index.php. Faculty of Forest and the Environment, Lakehead University, Canada
http://hua.huh.harvard.edu/FNA/. Flora of North America, United States
http://mobot.mobot.org/W3T/Search/vast.html. TROPICOS nomenclatural database, Missouri Botanical Garden
http://www.fs.fed.us/database/feis/index.html. USDA Forest Service

GINKGO FAMILY, GINKGOACEAE

Deciduous
Up to 100ft

J	F	M	A	M	J
J	A	S	O	N	D

ID FACT FILE

CROWN
Conical, irregular

BARK
Gray, becoming
furrowed

TWIGS
Greenish-brown,
stout, spurred

LEAVES
Scattered or
in clusters,
5×4in, fan-
shaped, usually
deeply 2-lobed,
leathery

FLOWERS
Males, yellowish
in erect catkins,
females paired,
on separate
trees

FRUITS
1¼in, oval,
green ripening
yellow, fleshy,
foul-smelling

Maidenhair Tree (Ginkgo)
Ginkgo biloba

Ginkgo is the sole survivor of an ancient lineage of trees, other species only being known from fossils. Most closely related to conifers but in its own distinct family, it is native to China, although now possibly extinct in the wild. It is widely grown in eastern and western states as a large specimen tree with attractive fanlike foliage. The unpleasant-smelling fruits are eaten in China.

PINE FAMILY, PINACEAE

Evergreen
Up to 80ft

| J | F | M | A | M | J |
| J | A | S | O | N | D |

Balsam Fir
Abies balsamea

This tree is largely found north of the United States in Canada, and is the only northeastern fir species. In the United States it ranges from Minnesota south to Iowa, east to Pennsylvania, and south through the Appalachians to Virginia. A relatively common, although short-lived tree, it is used for pulpwood and is also grown for use as a Christmas tree. Resin blisters on the bark yield a resin known as Canada Balsam, used for mounting microscope slides.

ID FACT FILE

CROWN
Pyramidal

BARK
Brown, smooth with many resin blisters, becoming scaly

TWIGS
Slender, hairy

LEAVES
Needle-like, ½–1in, curved, shiny green above with whitish bands below, spreading in 2 rows

CONES
2–3in, cylindrical, erect and purplish on upper twigs, cone scales with fine hairs

PINE FAMILY, PINACEAE

Evergreen
Up to 50ft

| J | F | M | A | M | J |
| J | A | S | O | N | D |

Fraser Fir
Abies fraseri

ID FACT FILE

CROWN
Pyramidal

BARK
Gray-brown,
smooth with
many resin
blisters,
becoming
scaly

TWIGS
Slender, hairy

LEAVES
Needle-like,
½–1in, flattened,
curved, shiny
green above
with 2 whitish
bands below,
spreading in
2 rows

CONES
1½–2½in,
cylindrical,
erect and
purplish on
upper twigs,
cone scales
with fine hairs

Fraser Fir is closely related to Balsam
Fir but is found in the southeast, in the
Appalachian Mountains of Virginia, North
Carolina, and Tennessee, where it is often
found growing with Red Spruce (*Picea
rubens*). Like Balsam Fir, this species also
possesses resin blisters on the bark but Fraser
Fir is much more commonly used for
ornamental use, and is also widely grown as
a Christmas tree.

PINE FAMILY, PINACEAE

Deciduous
Up to 80ft

J	F	M	A	M	J
J	A	S	O	N	D

Tamarack
Larix laricina

Tamarack is found only in the very northeast of the United States, as far west as Minnesota with local populations in Virginia and Maryland. It extends much farther north into Canada and Alaska where it can be seen up to the timber line. It has a strong preference for acidic boggy conditions and is generally slow-growing. The timber is durable and of some use as lumber or pulp.

ID FACT FILE

CROWN
Conical

BARK
Reddish-brown, scaly

TWIGS
Brown, stout, hairless, spurred

LEAVES
Needle-like, flattened, 1in, scattered and alternate on long shoots, crowded in clusters on spur shoots, blue-green turning yellow in autumn

CONES
½–¾in, elliptical, erect, cone scales rounded, overlapping, reddish maturing brown

PINE FAMILY, PINACEAE

Evergreen
Up to 80ft

J	F	M	A	M	J
J	A	S	O	N	D

Red Spruce
Picea rubens

ID FACT FILE

CROWN
Narrow, conical

BARK
Reddish-brown,
becoming darker
and deeply
furrowed

TWIGS
Brown, hairy

LEAVES
Needle-like,
½–⅝in, pointed,
yellow-green
above, with
whitish bands,
radiating on
shoots, borne on
short pegs

CONES
1–2in,
cylindrical,
reddish-brown,
pendulous, cone
scales rounded

Red Spruce is restricted to the northeast of the
United States, from New England south along
the Appalachians to North Carolina and
Tennessee, although it is also found in the
southeast of Canada. Large native forests still
occur, although the tree is widely harvested for
lumber and pulp. It is also used in forest
regeneration projects and was formerly
exploited for making chewing gum from resin
in the trunk, and spruce beer from the foliage.
Although it is a handsome tree, it is not widely
grown ornamentally.

PINE FAMILY, PINACEAE

Evergreen
Up to 100ft

J	F	M	A	M	J
J	A	S	O	N	D

White Spruce
Picea glauca

ID FACT FILE

CROWN
Narrowly conical

BARK
Gray to brown,
smooth
becoming scaly

TWIGS
Reddish-brown,
slender, hairless

LEAVES
Needle-like,
flattened, ½–¾in,
4-angled,
stiff, pointed,
spreading on
upper side
of twig, blue-
green with white
bands, smelling
unpleasant when
crushed, borne
on short pegs

CONES
1½–2½in,
cylindrical, brown,
pendulous when
mature, cone
scales rounded

White Spruce is one of the most widely
distributed conifer species across North
America. Found across the breadth of the
north of the continent from Alaska to the east
of Canada, south into Maine and Minnesota
with isolated populations in Montana, the
Dakotas and Wyoming. In its native range it is
one of the most important timber trees used
for construction and is also widely used in
reforestation and as a shelterbelt tree. In
common with *P. engelmannii*, the resonant
wood is also used to make musical instruments.

PINE FAMILY, PINACEAE

Evergreen
Up to 60ft

Black Spruce
Picea mariana

ID FACT FILE

CROWN
Narrowly conical, with lower branches drooping

BARK
Dark gray, becoming scaly

TWIGS
Reddish-brown, slender, hairy

LEAVES
Needle-like, flattened, ⅜–⅝in, 4-angled, stiff, pointed, spreading, blue-green with white bands, borne on short pegs

CONES
½–1¼in, egg-shaped, curved, brown, pendulous when mature, remaining on tree for many years, cone scales toothed

This species, like White Spruce, is also transcontinental across Canada to Alaska, although only ranging south as far as New Jersey and Minnesota. It is also used for much the same range of uses as the related *P. glauca*, although is more limited as a construction timber due to its smaller size. It grows easily from seed but also propagates itself by layering where the lower branches, weighed down by snow, take root in the ground. Often in bogs known as muskegs.

Evergreen
Up to 70ft

Jack Pine
Pinus banksiana

ID FACT FILE

CROWN
Open, irregular

BARK
Reddish-brown, scaly, becoming ridged and fissured

TWIGS
Greenish-brown, resinous

LEAVES
Needle-like, 1–1½in, slender, in pairs, often twisted, yellow-green

CONES
2–3in, irregularly cylindrical, pointed at tip, yellow-brown, cone scales rounded, often persistent for many years

The Jack Pine is found across Canada east of the Rocky Mountains, but only found in eastern United States from Maine and New Hampshire in the east, west to Indiana and Minnesota. Jack Pine is one of the northernmost occurring pine species, extending almost to the Arctic in the Canadian north. It is a colonizing species and an important tree for wildlife, especially a rare species of warbler, only found nesting in young, large, pure stands of Jack Pine. This species, named after the famous botanical explorer, Sir Joseph Banks, is also an important commercial tree, mainly for lumber and pulpwood, but is also occasionally planted for use as Christmas trees.

PINE FAMILY, PINACEAE

Evergreen
Up to 100ft

| J | F | M | A | M | J |
| J | A | S | O | N | D |

Shortleaf Pine
Pinus echinata

ID FACT FILE

CROWN
Broad, open

BARK
Reddish-brown,
furrowed into
irregular plates

TWIGS
Brown, hairy
when young

LEAVES
Needle-like,
3–5in, flexible, in
clusters of 2 or
3, blue-green

CONES
1½–2½in,
conical, brown, in
small clusters,
cone scales
raised, with
small spine,
often persistent
for many years

Widely distributed across the southeastern
states, Shortleaf Pine is found from New York
to Florida and westward as far as Texas and
Missouri, in a variety of soils and habitats.
It is one of the important commercial timber
trees of the southeast and is used for lumber
for construction materials and other uses.
Although the cones release their seed upon
maturity, the seeds will often not germinate
until after fire, and the tree itself has the
ability to resprout from the base if burned
in forest fires.

PINE FAMILY, PINACEAE

Evergreen
Up to 100ft

| J | F | M | A | M | J |
| J | A | S | O | N | D |

Slash Pine
Pinus elliotii

ID FACT FILE

CROWN
Conical,
becoming
open and
rounded

BARK
Orange-brown,
darkening with
age and
becoming scaly

TWIGS
Brown, hairy
when young

LEAVES
Needle-like,
7–10in, stiff, in
clusters of
2 or 3, glossy,
green

CONES
2½–6in, conical,
brown, shiny,
cone scales with
small spine

A fast-growing colonizing tree, often found
in pure stands especially in areas which have
been burned, Slash Pine is found across the
coastal plain from South California to Florida
and west to Louisiana. It is an important
habitat tree in the wild and is also sometimes
grown ornamentally. However, its greatest
importance is as a timber tree and it is
extensively grown in plantations for lumber,
both within and north of its natural range.

PINE FAMILY, PINACEAE

Evergreen
Up to 100ft

J	F	M	A	M	J
J	A	S	O	N	D

Longleaf Pine
Pinus palustris

In common with the western Apache Pine (*P. engelmannii*), seedlings of this species go through a transitional grasslike stage. It is a potentially long-lived tree, found along the eastern coastal plain from Virginia to Florida and Texas and shows a distinct preference for acidic, sandy soils where it is often seen in pure stands at low elevations. It is an important timber for naval stores and it is also tapped for its resin and turpentine.

ID FACT FILE

CROWN
Open, irregular

BARK
Gray, becoming orange-brown, furrowed and scaly

TWIGS
Brown, ending in distinctive large, white buds

LEAVES
Needle-like, 8–16in, drooping, in dense clusters of 3, dark green

CONES
6–10in, conical, brown, usually in clusters, cone scales raised, with small spine

PINE FAMILY, PINACEAE

Evergreen
Up to 40ft

J	F	M	A	M	J
J	A	S	O	N	D

Table Mountain Pine
Pinus pungens

ID FACT FILE

CROWN
Rounded
to irregular

BARK
Dark brown,
fissured and
scaly

TWIGS
Orange-brown

LEAVES
Needle-like,
1¼–2½in,
spreading, in
clusters of 2 or
3, dark green

CONES
2½–4in, oval,
reddish-brown,
usually in
clusters, cone
scales thick,
with curved spine

Restricted to the Appalachian Mountains from Pennsylvania to Georgia with localized populations also found in Delaware and New York, Table Mountain Pine normally grows at high elevations on ridges and rocky slopes. The common name derives from the strong branches which somewhat resemble those of hickory species. It is a useful tree for erosion control on steep slopes and of value as a habitat tree but is otherwise not much used.

PINE FAMILY, PINACEAE

Evergreen
Up to 80ft

| J | F | M | A | M | J |
| J | A | S | O | N | D |

Red Pine
Pinus resinosa

ID FACT FILE

CROWN
Conical,
becoming
rounded or
spreading
and irregular

BARK
Reddish-brown,
with large scaly
plates, becoming
thickly furrowed

TWIGS
Reddish, slender

LEAVES
Needle-like,
4–6in, slender,
in pairs, pointed,
shiny dark green

CONES
1½–2½in, egg-
shaped, shiny
brown, usually
in pairs, cone
scales thick,
spineless

Intensely harvested for timber and pulp, this
species has relatively few old pure stands in the
wild. Native to the Great Lakes region of the
northeast, it is now widely planted as a forestry
tree and used in shelterbelts. In common with
many other Pine species, it is used in avalanche
and erosion control. Favoring open conditions,
it is largely dependent on fire to remove more
competitive tree species in order for it to thrive.

PINE FAMILY, PINACEAE

Evergreen
Up to 65ft

J	F	M	A	M	J
J	A	S	O	N	D

Pitch Pine
Pinus rigida

ID FACT FILE

CROWN
Rounded or irregular

BARK
Reddish-brown, furrowed, with large irregular plates

TWIGS
Reddish, slender

LEAVES
Needle-like, 3–5in, slender, in threes, twisted, pointed, shiny yellow-green

CONES
1¼–3in, egg-shaped, yellow-brown, usually in pairs, cone scales thick, with recurved spine

Pitch Pine is so called on account of the large amounts of resin within the knotty wood. For this reason, it was formerly used as a source of tar and turpentine, although it is now most widely grown as a lumber tree. Fast-growing but short-lived, it is highly adapted to fire, and has the ability to resprout from the trunk after a fire, often forming a multistemmed tree. It is native to the northeast, from Maine south to Georgia and west to Ohio, and also southeastern Canada.

PINE FAMILY, PINACEAE

Evergreen
Up to 150ft

J	F	M	A	M	J
J	A	S	O	N	D

Eastern White Pine
Pinus strobus

A large tree highly valued for its soft, versatile timber, the Eastern White Pine is intensively harvested in its natural range from the Great Lakes north into Canada. Although potentially attaining a height of 150ft or more, wild individuals over 100ft are now rare as a direct result of its exploitation for timber. It is easily distinguished from other pines by the tuft of hairs found at the base of each bundle of needles.

ID FACT FILE

CROWN
Conical, becoming irregular and open with horizontal, spreading branches

BARK
Gray-green, smooth, becoming gray-brown, thick, fissured, and scaly

TWIGS
Gray-green, slender

LEAVES
Needle-like, 2–4½in, slender, in fives, blue-green, with tuft of hairs at base on young shoots

CONES
3¼–8in, cylindrical, yellow-brown, cone scales thin, rounded

PINE FAMILY, PINACEAE

Scots Pine
Pinus sylvestris

Evergreen
Up to 120ft

J	F	M	A	M	J
J	A	S	O	N	D

ID FACT FILE

CROWN
Rounded and spreading, becoming irregular and flat-topped

BARK
Reddish-brown and scaly lower down, paler and papery higher up

TWIGS
Reddish-brown, slender

LEAVES
Needle-like, 1–3in, slender, in pairs, twisted, blue-green

CONES
1–3in, egg-shaped, in clusters, reddish-brown, ripening gray in second year, cone scales flat, with a small spine

This species is native across Europe, although now much reduced in range, and introduced across the United States as a shelterbelt and ornamental tree, where it has become naturalized in many areas in the northeast. Scots Pine is a useful timber tree and is important for wildlife in its native habitat; in the United States, native species better fulfill these purposes although young trees are often used as Christmas trees.

PINE FAMILY, PINACEAE

Evergreen
Up to 100ft

J	F	M	A	M	J
J	A	S	O	N	D

Loblolly Pine
Pinus taeda

ID FACT FILE

CROWN
Pyramidal

BARK
Gray-black,
becoming
reddish-brown,
furrowed and
scaly

TWIGS
Orange-brown,
hairy when young

LEAVES
Needle-like,
5–9in, twisted,
usually in
clusters of 3,
sometimes 2,
yellow-green

CONES
Up to 6in,
conical, brown,
cone scales
thick, with sharp
spine

Naturally found in wetland areas bordering rivers and floodplains, the Loblolly Pine also extends to moist, upland soils. It has an extensive distribution across many eastern states, from New Jersey to Florida, and west to Texas and Oklahoma. It is the major commercial pine of the southeast and is extensively grown in plantations for lumber. It is a very fast-growing and variable tree, quick to colonize disturbed areas and become established, although it is not adapted to areas experiencing forest fires.

PINE FAMILY, PINACEAE

Evergreen
Up to 60ft

J	F	M	A	M	J
J	A	S	O	N	D

Virginia Pine
Pinus virginiana

ID FACT FILE

CROWN
Open, irregular

BARK
Gray-brown,
smooth,
becoming ridged
and fissured

TWIGS
Greenish-brown,
with a glaucous
bloom

LEAVES
Needle-like,
1½–3in, slender,
in pairs, often
twisted, gray-
green

CONES
1½–3in, conical,
reddish-brown,
cone scales
rounded, with
small spine,
often persistent
for many years
although maturing
in one season

Virginia Pine somewhat resembles Jack Pine
(*Pinus banksiana*), to which it is closely related.
It is found generally at low elevations from
Long Island in the north, south through the
Appalachian Mountains to northern Mississippi,
and north to Indiana. Often seen in pure
stands—especially as a colonizing species on
derilect farmland—it is also seen in mixed forests
although it is intolerant of shade. Of little
commercial use beyond as pulp, it is
nevertheless an important tree both for wildlife
and in the colonization of poor and
impoverished soils such as abandoned farmland.

PINE FAMILY, PINACEAE

Evergreen
Up to 70ft

| J | F | M | A | M | J |
| J | A | S | O | N | D |

Carolina Hemlock
Tsuga caroliniana

ID FACT FILE

CROWN
Conical

BARK
Reddish-brown,
deeply furrowed,
and ridged

TWIGS
Reddish-brown,
slender with
peglike base

LEAVES
Needle-like,
½–¾in, arranged
radially, flattened,
blunt, shiny-green
above, paler with
two whitish bands
below, aromatic

CONES
Up to 1½in,
elliptical, brown,
drooping, cone
scales spreading

The rarest of the American hemlocks, Carolina Hemlock is restricted to mixed hardwood and coniferous forests of the slopes of the southern Appalachians. It is only found from southern Virginia, south to northern Georgia. It is an attractive tree with slightly drooping branches, and is often grown ornamentally. In common with other *Tsuga* species, the crushed foliage is reported to have a similar fragrance to the infamous herb, Hemlock (*Conium maculatum*), of Eurasia.

CYPRESS FAMILY, CUPRESSACEAE

Evergreen
Up to 80ft

| J | F | M | A | M | J |
| J | A | S | O | N | D |

Atlantic White Cedar
Chamaecyparis thyoides

ID FACT FILE

CROWN
Spire-like

BARK
Reddish-brown,
fibrous becoming
scaly

TWIGS
Slender,
flattened

LEAVES
Scale-like, in
opposite,
spreading, pairs,
⅛in, pressed
tightly to the
shoot, blue-green
with whitish dots

CONES
Tiny, up to ¼in,
rounded, reddish-
brown, scales 6,
pointed

A coastal species found in a narrow strip along
the Eastern Seaboard from Maine to Florida and
west to Mississippi, usually in wet acidic soils. It is
a long-lived species (up to 1,000 years) and the
fragrant timber is highly valued for its extremely
durable qualities, being resistant to decay even
in wet conditions. As a consequence, trees are
extensively used in habitat restoration in
wetland sites. The species is also widely grown
as a stately ornamental specimen in appropriate
sites and various cultivars are sold commercially.

CYPRESS FAMILY, CUPRESSACEAE

Evergreen
Up to 20ft

Common Juniper
Juniperus communis

ID FACT FILE

CROWN
Spreading

BARK
Reddish-brown,
scaly and
shredding

TWIGS
Pale, slender,
hairless

LEAVES
Needle-like,
prickly, flattened
in whorls of 3,
⅜–1¼in, bluish-
green with white
band above,
yellow-green
below

CONES
¼–⅜in, fleshy,
berrylike,
globular, whitish-
blue ripening
blue-black in
second or third
year

This is an extremely widespread species found
through Eurasia and across North America in
an arc containing much of Canada then south
through east-central US states (New York to
Minnesota) to South Carolina. It also ranges
south from west-central Canada along the
Rocky Mountains to Wyoming and Arizona. It
is a variable species ranging from a small tree in
the eastern states, to a low-growing shrub in the
west, often at high elevations. There are many
cultivated varieties varying in form and color.
As well as being cultivated ornamentally, the
fruits are also exploited medicinally and are
also used for flavouring drinks and food.
However, care is needed since the fruits are in
fact poisonous in large doses.

CYPRESS FAMILY, CUPRESSACEAE

Evergreen
Up to 100ft

J	F	M	A	M	J
J	A	S	O	N	D

Eastern Red Cedar
Juniperus virginiana

ID FACT FILE

CROWN
Pyramidal

BARK
Reddish-brown, fibrous and shredding

TWIGS
Rounded, scaly

LEAVES
Juvenile foliage needle-like, 3-ranked, ¼in, bluish-green above, green below, adult foliage scale-like, paired, ¹⁄₁₆in, pressed close to the shoot, green

CONES
⅛in, fleshy, berrylike, globular, blue with a bloom ripening blue-black in second year

The most widely distributed conifer found in the United States—found throughout the East as far west as Texas to Dakota in the north—Eastern Red Cedar occurs in a range of habitats from floodplains to dry uplands. The aromatic timber has long been exploited for a variety of uses including the wood for pencils, hence the common name. Other uses include as a windbreak and in landscape restoration. There are also many ornamental cultivated varieties.

CYPRESS FAMILY, CUPRESSACEAE

Deciduous
Up to 70ft

J	F	M	A	M	J
J	A	S	O	N	D

Pond Cypress
Taxodium ascendens

ID FACT FILE

CROWN
Pyramidal

BARK
Reddish-brown,
peeling in fibrous
strips

TWIGS
Brown, densely
covered with
foliage

LEAVES
Needle or scale-
like, ¼–½in,
arranged spirally
on leading
shoots, on
young shoots
in 2 rows, pale
green above,
turning orange-
brown in autumn

CONES
Up to 1¼in,
rounded, yellow-
green ripening
brown, at ends
of twigs, cone
scales 4-angled
with short spine

Pond Cypress is often treated as a smaller
variety of Bald Cypress (*T. distichum*) but
differing in some physical characteristics and
also in its habitat preference. It is found within
the range of Bald Cypress, but is restricted to
the coastal plain from Virginia, south to
Florida, and west to Louisiana. It tends to be
found near shallow ponds or depressions in
more acidic soils, and also has smaller leaves
on more erect branches. It also produces
pneumatophores but to a lesser degree, and
they also tend to be smaller than those of the
closely related Bald Cypress.

CYPRESS FAMILY, CUPRESSACEAE

Deciduous
Up to 165ft

J	F	M	A	M	J
J	A	S	O	N	D

Bald Cypress
Taxodium distichum

ID FACT FILE

CROWN
Triangular, spreading

BARK
Reddish-brown, peeling in fibrous strips

TWIGS
Greenish, slender

LEAVES
Needle-like, ⅜–⅞in, arranged spirally on leading shoots, elsewhere in 2 rows, pale green above, whitish below, turning orange-brown in autumn

CONES
½–1¼in, rounded, gray ripening purple, at ends of twigs, cone scales 4-angled with short spine

Bald Cypress is found in swampy areas in the southeastern United States from Delaware to Florida and west to Texas and Indiana in the North. Although tolerant of drier ground, it is usually found in swamps or other moist areas where it produces prominently raised stumplike roots called pneumatophores, which enable the tree to "breathe" when the base is submerged. It is also widely grown as an ornamental tree and produces attractive orange-brown autumn foliage.

CYPRESS FAMILY, CUPRESSACEAE

Evergreen
Up to 70ft

J	F	M	A	M	J
J	A	S	O	N	D

Northern White Cedar
Thuja occidentalis

ID FACT FILE

CROWN
Narrow, conical with enlarged buttressed base

BARK
Reddish-brown, shallowly fissured, and shredding

TWIGS
Flattened, densely clothed with scales, branching

LEAVES
Scale-like, ⅛in, arranged in flattened sprays, in 4 rows, pointed, resinous, yellow-green

CONES
Up to ½in, elliptical, in erect clusters, ripening brown, cone scales 8–10, paired, with short spine

Northern White Cedar has an extensive distribution in southeast Canada and, in the United States, is found from Maine through New York and west to Illinois, Wisconsin, and Minnesota. Localized populations are also known in the Appalachian Mountains of Georgia and Tennessee. It is an extensively exploited tree, the timber is used for lumber and poles, and the twigs are the source of a medicinal oil. It is also widely grown ornamentally and many cultivated forms have been developed, including prostrate and variegated forms.

MAGNOLIA FAMILY, MAGNOLIACEAE

Deciduous
Up to 150ft

J	F	M	A	M	J
J	A	S	O	N	D

Tulip Tree
Liriodendron tulipifera

ID FACT FILE

Crown
Narrow,
becoming
spreading

Bark
Gray-brown,
becoming thick
and furrowed

Twigs
Brown, hairless

Leaves
Alternate, 3–6in,
4–6 spreading,
paired lobes with
the 2 at the apex
only shallowly
lobed so that the
tip is a broad,
notched, V-shape,
dark shiny green
above, paler
below

Flowers
1½–2in,
cup-shaped with
3 outer greenish
petals and 6
inner petals,
yellow and
orange, solitary,
erect

Fruits
Narrow, conelike
to 3in, brown

The Tulip Tree is a fast-growing, long-lived specimen tree favoring moist, well-drained soils and found usually as an isolated tree though sometimes in pure stands. It occurs naturally from Michigan and Vermont in the north, south to Florida and Louisiana, where it may be found at higher elevations. It is also widely grown ornamentally and is a valued timber tree. The common name refers to the flowers, which are tuliplike when young, although the foliage, the leaves of which look as though they have been cut at the tip, is also particularly impressive in autumn.

MAGNOLIA FAMILY, MAGNOLIACEAE

Deciduous
Up to 80ft

| J | F | M | A | M | J |
| J | A | S | O | N | D |

Cucumber Tree
Magnolia acuminata

ID FACT FILE

CROWN
Broad, spreading

BARK
Gray-brown,
ridged and scaly

TWIGS
Densely hairy
when young

LEAVES
Alternate,
5–10in, elliptical,
wavy-edged, shiny
dark green
above, paler and
softly hairy
below, turning
yellow
in autumn

FLOWERS
2½–3½in,
solitary, bell-
shaped, yellow

FRUITS
2½–3in,
conelike,
reddish-brown,
composed of
many individual
pointed fruits

Found in small groups or as individuals on lower mountain slopes and along river valleys, Cucumber Tree is the northernmost of the magnolias. In the United States it ranges from New York south to Florida, west to Louisiana, and north along the Mississippi River to Missouri. It is occasionally seen as an ornamental tree but otherwise the species is not much used, the wood produced being soft and not very strong.

MAGNOLIA FAMILY, MAGNOLIACEAE

Southern Magnolia
Magnolia grandiflora

Evergreen
Up to 100ft

| J | F | M | A | M | J |
| J | A | S | O | N | D |

ID FACT FILE

CROWN
Conical, branches spreading

BARK
Gray, smooth, becoming furrowed and scaly

TWIGS
Covered with reddish hairs when young

LEAVES
Alternate, 3¼–6½in, elliptical, wavy-edged, leathery, shiny dark green above, pale with reddish hairs below

FLOWERS
6–10in, solitary, cup-shaped, white

FRUITS
2–2½in, conelike, brown, covered with reddish hairs

The Southern Magnolia is a large spreading evergreen tree naturally found from North Carolina to Florida and Texas in the west. Although sometimes taking many years to reach flowering size, it is now grown all over the world in temperate climes as a beautiful shade or ornamental tree, and there are several cultivated forms. It benefits from lustrous green foliage and a prolonged flowering season, the fragrant flowers appearing in spring and continuing throughout the summer.

Deciduous
Up to 40ft

J	F	M	A	M	J
J	A	S	O	N	D

Bigleaf Magnolia
Magnolia macrophylla

ID FACT FILE

CROWN
Broad, rounded

BARK
Gray, smooth

TWIGS
Densely whitish-hairy

LEAVES
Alternate,
12–30in,
elliptical, wavy-edged, green
above, paler and
whitish-hairy
below

FLOWERS
10–12in,
solitary, cup-shaped, creamy-white, fragrant

FRUITS
2½–3in, conelike,
reddish-brown,
composed of
many individual
pointed fruits

Bigleaf Magnolia is naturally found from
North Carolina south to Georgia and west to
Louisiana. Small, isolated populations are also
known in Ohio, Arkansas, and South Carolina.
It is a relatively small understory tree of mixed
deciduous woodlands but is also sometimes
planted as an ornamental for its large-leaved
foliage and fragrant flowers, as far north as
Massachussets. In cultivation, however, it
needs protection from the wind which will
otherwise tear the large, attractive foliage.

MAGNOLIA FAMILY, MAGNOLIACEAE

Umbrella Magnolia
Magnolia tripetala

Deciduous
Up to 40ft

J	F	M	A	M	J
J	A	S	O	N	D

ID FACT FILE

CROWN
Open, broad

BARK
Gray, smooth

TWIGS
Greenish-brown

LEAVES
Alternate,
10–20in, oval,
green above,
paler and whitish-
hairy below
when young,
unpleasant-
smelling

FLOWERS
7–10in, solitary,
cup-shaped,
greenish-white,
unpleasant-
smelling

FRUITS
2½–4in, conelike,
pinkish-red,
composed of
many individual
pointed fruits

The leaves of this magnolia clustered together at the ends of the twigs give an umbrella-like appearance, from which the tree derives its common name. The Umbrella Magnolia is naturally found from Pennsylvania south to Georgia and west to Mississippi, and north to Indiana; there are also small scattered populations further west. The foliage and flowers smell unpleasant and hence it is not widely grown as an ornamental tree despite the attractive habit provided by the arrangement of the leaves.

MAGNOLIA FAMILY, MAGNOLIACEAE

Semi-Evergreen
Up to 60ft

| J | F | M | A | M | J |
| J | A | S | O | N | D |

Sweetbay Magnolia
Magnolia virginiana

A wetland species favoring riverbanks and streams, Sweetbay Magnolia is also found in coastal swamps along the Eastern Seaboard, from Massachussets in the north to Florida and Texas in the south. It tends to attain greater stature in the south, where it is also virtually evergreen. It is widely planted outside of its natural range as an ornamental tree on account of its relatively small manageable size, attractive foliage, and fragrant flowers.

ID FACT FILE

CROWN
Narrow, rounded

BARK
Gray, smooth

TWIGS
Greenish-brown, with buds covered in whitish hairs

LEAVES
Alternate, 3–6in, oval, thickened, shiny-green above, paler and whitish-hairy below

FLOWERS
2–2½in, solitary, cup-shaped, creamy-white, fragrant

FRUITS
1½–2in, conelike, red, composed of many individual pointed fruits

CUSTARD APPLE FAMILY, ANNONACEAE

Deciduous
Up to 33ft

J	F	M	A	M	J
J	A	S	O	N	D

Pawpaw
Asimina triloba

ID FACT FILE

CROWN
Spreading

BARK
Brown, warty

TWIGS
Reddish-brown, hairy

LEAVES
Alternate, 7–10in, ovate, narrowed at base, green above, paler below, hairy when young, turning yellow in autumn

FLOWERS
Up to 1½in, with 3 inner and 3 outer petals arranged in a triangular fashion, overlapping, purple

FRUITS
Up to 5½in, cylindrical, berrylike, curved, yellow-green

The only species of a New World tropical family found so far north, with a wide but sporadic range from New York west to Nebraska and as far south as Texas and Florida. Other members of the family are harvested for their fruits as was Pawpaw in the past; today it is largely an animal food source, though many people do still gather and eat them. The bark was used by the Pioneers for medicinal properties. Both the flowers and fruits are very distinctive, the flowers because of their form and colour, and the fruits because of their taste, sometimes likened to a cross between apples and custard, hence the alternative common name, American Custard Apple.

LAUREL FAMILY, LAURACEAE

Deciduous
Up to 65ft

| J | F | M | A | M | J |
| J | A | S | O | N | D |

Sassafras
Sassafras albidum

A common small tree in eastern North America found from Maine south to Florida and west to Texas and north to Michigan, Sassafras is a species of sandy soils found in valleys and upland sites. The roots and root bark were once extensively used for medicinal properties and are the source of Sassafras oil, used to flavor root beer and tea. It often forms clumps where it spreads by suckers.

ID FACT FILE

CROWN
Narrow, spreading

BARK
Reddish-brown, thick, furrowed

TWIGS
Greenish, slender, aromatic

LEAVES
Alternate, 3–5in, elliptical, often variably lobed, long-pointed, shiny green above, paler and often hairy below, turning yellow, orange or red in autumn

FLOWERS
Small, to ½in, without petals, yellow-green, in clusters at ends of the twigs, males and females on separate trees

FRUITS
Up to ½in, berrylike, ripening blue-black with red cup

PLANE FAMILY, PLATANACEAE

Deciduous
Up to 100ft

J	F	M	A	M	J
J	A	S	O	N	D

Sycamore
Platanus occidentalis

A large, fast-growing, relatively long-lived tree with distinctive peeling, multicolored bark, Sycamore is a pioneer species. It is found throughout the eastern states from Maine and Nebraska in the north, to Texas and Florida in the south, developing an extremely large diameter trunk which may become hollow. The timber, if used, is largely restricted to pulpwood.

ID FACT FILE

CROWN
Broad, open, irregular

BARK
Gray, mottled white and brown, and smooth at first, peeling to become brown, green and gray mottled and furrowed at the base

TWIGS
Green, slender

LEAVES
Alternate, 4–8in, 3 or 5 shallow-lobed, lobes pointed, green, hairy when young, turning brown in autumn

FLOWERS
Tiny, greenish in single or paired clusters, males and females in separate clusters

FRUITS
1in, brown, ball-like head of plumed seeds

WITCH-HAZEL FAMILY, HAMAMELIDACEAE

Deciduous
Up to 30ft

J	F	M	A	M	J
J	A	S	O	N	D

Witch-Hazel
Hamamelis virginiana

ID FACT FILE

CROWN
Open, spreading

BARK
Brown, smooth

TWIGS
Slender, hairy

LEAVES
Alternate,
3¼–5in, elliptical,
unequal at base,
dark green
above, paler
below turning
yellow in autumn

FLOWERS
1in, in clusters
on leafless twigs,
4 threadlike
yellow petals

FRUITS
½in long,
elliptical, pale
brown, exploding
when ripe

Part of a widespread genus found in eastern
North America and East Asia, this species is
an understory tree found in mixed forests
throughout the eastern states as far south
as Florida and as far west as Wisconsin, and
Texas in the south. In common with other
species of the genus, extracts of the bark and
leaves have medicinal properties, and it was
formerly purported to have water-divining
properties. It is an attractive tree with
bright-yellow spidery flowers in fall.

WITCH-HAZEL FAMILY, HAMAMELIDACEAE

Deciduous
Up to 100ft

J	F	M	A	M	J
J	A	S	O	N	D

Sweetgum
Liquidambar styraciflua

ID FACT FILE

CROWN
Conical

BARK
Gray-brown,
fissured

TWIGS
Brown, stout,
often with
corklike wings

LEAVES
Alternate, 3–6in,
star-shaped with
5–7 deep,
pointed lobes,
dark green
turning red,
purple and yellow
in autumn

FLOWERS
Tiny, greenish,
males in
clusters, females
in pendent
clusters on same
tree

FRUITS
1in, globose,
prickly, brown

An attractive widespread tree, Sweetgum is common throughout eastern United States from Conneticut to Florida and west to Texas and Illinois. It also extends south into Mexico, Guatemala, and Belize, where it is found at high elevations. It is the source of an important commercial timber called Satinwood, and also "Storax"—a gum with medicinal properties. It is now also widely grown ornamentally across the United States, largely on account of its rich autumn color.

MULBERRY FAMILY, MORACEAE

Deciduous
Up to 50ft

| J | F | M | A | M | J |
| J | A | S | O | N | D |

Osage Orange
Maclura pomifera

ID FACT FILE

CROWN
Broad, rounded to irregular

BARK
Gray to brown, thick and furrowed into forking ridges

TWIGS
Brown, stout, with spines at nodes, spurred

LEAVES
Alternate, 2½–5in, oval, pointed at apex, shiny green above, paler below, turning yellow in autumn

FLOWERS
Tiny and inconspicuous, in dense clusters up to 1in, males and females on separate trees

FRUITS
4–5in, globular, fleshy ball, greenish-yellow

This utilitarian tree was originally found from Arkansas to Texas, but is now widely planted in eastern and northwestern states. Prior to the advent of barbed wire, it was much used in the Midwest for fencing because it has spines growing at nodes along the branches and shoots. A yellow dye can be extracted from the roots and the wood was previously used to construct bows, giving rise to the alternative common name, "Bowwood."

MULBERRY FAMILY, MORACEAE

Deciduous
Up to 50ft

J	F	M	A	M	J
J	A	S	O	N	D

White Mulberry
Morus alba

Originally native to China, this species was introduced to the United States and over several centuries has become naturalized in both eastern and western states. In its native habitat, the leaves are used as a foodstuff for silkworms in farms although in the United States it is primarily grown as an ornamental tree. Several cultivated forms exist, grown either for their flowers or habit. It is a common urban tree.

ID FACT FILE

CROWN
Narrow, rounded

BARK
Gray, smooth becoming deeply ridged

TWIGS
Slender, hairy when young

LEAVES
Alternate, 2½–7in, oval, toothed, green above, paler and hairy below

FLOWERS
Tiny, greenish, in erect clusters, males and females on the same or separate trees

FRUITS
½–¾in, compound fruit, cylindrical, white, pink or purple, sweet-tasting

MULBERRY FAMILY, MORACEAE

Deciduous
Up to 60ft

J	F	M	A	M	J
J	A	S	O	N	D

Red Mulberry
Morus rubra

ID FACT FILE

CROWN
Broad, rounded

BARK
Reddish-brown,
smooth with
lenticels when
young, becoming
fissured and
scaly

TWIGS
Brown, slender

LEAVES
Alternate, 4–8in,
oval, long-
pointed at apex,
coarsely toothed,
sometimes lobed,
dull green above,
hairy below,
turning yellow
in autumn

FLOWERS
Tiny, greenish,
in erect clusters,
males and
females on
the same or
separate trees

FRUITS
1in, compound
fruit, cylindrical,
red or purple,
sweet-tasting

An adaptable tree, Red Mulberry is found on prairies, in woodland, and along forest edges from Massachussets to Minnesota in the north, south to Texas and Florida; it is also cultivated in western states. The wood is weak but used locally for fenceposts and to an extent, furniture. The fruits are popular with birds and animals and people alike, but the species is very susceptible to a variety of diseases in cultivation.

ELM FAMILY, ULMACEAE

Deciduous
Up to 90ft

J	F	M	A	M	J
J	A	S	O	N	D

Common Hackberry
Celtis occidentalis

ID FACT FILE

CROWN
Rounded, spreading

BARK
Gray, developing corky ridges

TWIGS
Slender, brown, hairy

LEAVES
Alternate, 2–5in, oval with pointed tip, unequal base, toothed, green and smooth above, paler and hairy below, turning yellow in autumn

FLOWERS
Tiny, up to ⅛in, males and females both greenish occurring at base of young leaves

FRUITS
¼–½in, orange-red to purple drupe, sweet

Found across the eastern states from New England and Dakota in the north, south to Oklahoma and Georgia in the south. Scattered populations are also found in Virginia and other areas. Hackberry develops distinctive warty bark in old age but is an attractive drought-tolerant tree of great ecological importance for local birds, mammals, and insects. It is also extensively planted as a windbreak due to its spreading habit and deep roots, and the timber is also used as a fuel wood.

Deciduous
Up to 80ft

J	F	M	A	M	J
J	A	S	O	N	D

ELM FAMILY, ULMACEAE

Sugarberry
Celtis laevigata

ID FACT FILE

CROWN
Rounded, open

BARK
Gray, smooth, becoming warty

TWIGS
Slender, green, hairless

LEAVES
Alternate, 2½–4in, lanceolate, pointed at apex, unequal base, green above, paler below, turning yellow in autumn

FLOWERS
Tiny, up to ⅛in, males and females both greenish, occurring at base of young leaves

FRUITS
Up to ⅓in, orange-red to purple drupe, sweet

A southern tree favoring humid low-lying areas, this species is found in scattered populations from Virginia and Florida, west to Texas and Illinois. It is a successional tree, replacing other colonizing species although ultimately, being replaced itself in turn by more competitive species. Slow-growing, it has some use as an ornamental tree and the wood is also used in flooring and furniture. The sweet fruits are a favored food source of many birds.

ELM FAMILY, ULMACEAE

Deciduous
Up to 30ft

| J | F | M | A | M | J |
| J | A | S | O | N | D |

Netleaf Hackberry
Celtis reticulata

ID FACT FILE

CROWN
Spreading, irregular

BARK
Gray, thick, becoming warty and scaly

TWIGS
Slender, reddish-brown, usually hairy though sometimes hairless

LEAVES
Alternate, 1¼–2½in, variably lanceolate to oval, pointed at apex, unequal base, green and rough above, paler and distinctly veined below

FLOWERS
Tiny, up to ⅛in, males and females both greenish, occurring at base of young leaves

FRUITS
Up to ⅜in, orange-red drupe, sweet

Found in the southern central states of Kansas, Oklahoma, and Texas, and also ranging westward to southern California and Washington, this native hackberry favors moist sites although it can to an extent, also tolerate drought conditions. The common name derives from the fine netlike veination of the lower surface of the leaves, the upper surface of which are rough to the touch. The sweet fruits are much consumed by wildlife and were also formerly used by people as a food source. This slow-growing species is also an important habitat tree for wildlife, providing ideal nesting for many birds.

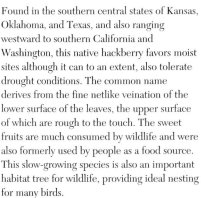

ELM FAMILY, ULMACEAE

Winged Elm
Ulmus alata

Deciduous
Up to 80ft

J	F	M	A	M	J
J	A	S	O	N	D

ID FACT FILE

CROWN
Open

BARK
Pale brown,
furrowed

TWIGS
Brown, with two
broad corky
wings

LEAVES
Alternate,
1½–2½in, in 2
rows, oval,
toothed, dark
green above,
paler and hairy
below, turning
yellow and red in
autumn

FLOWERS
Appearing before
the leaves, tiny,
greenish, without
petals, in
clusters

FRUITS
Up to ½in,
elliptical,
flattened,
reddish-brown,
hairy, with a
narrow wing

Occasionally grown as an ornamental tree, Winged Elm is an attractive species with good autumn color. In the wild it is found in a mixture of hardwood forests, and also as a colonizing species, on moist soils and ranges from Virginia south to Florida, west to Texas and north to Missouri, although it is absent from the lower Mississippi delta. The wood is used to an extent, and the fibrous inner bark was formerly used to make rope.

ELM FAMILY, ULMACEAE

Deciduous
Up to 100ft

J	F	M	A	M	J
J	A	S	O	N	D

American Elm
Ulmus americana

ID FACT FILE

CROWN
Broadly rounded, flat-topped

BARK
Gray, furrowed and ridged

TWIGS
Brown, hairless

LEAVES
Alternate, 3–6in, in 2 rows, oval, pointed, toothed, dark green and smooth above, paler and hairy below, turning yellow in autumn

FLOWERS
Appearing before the leaves, tiny, greenish, without petals, in clusters

FRUITS
Up to ½in, elliptical, flattened, reddish-brown, ciliate, with a narrow wing

This once common and abundant elm has a wide, predominantly eastern distribution, although it is found as far west as Montana and Wyoming, occurring roughly east of a line from eastern Montana to Texas. It also ranges across southeastern Canada. It has been very adversely affected by the introduction of Dutch Elm disease, which has wiped out both urban plantings and wild populations, although disease-resistant forms are now commercially available.

ELM FAMILY, ULMACEAE

Deciduous
Up to 80ft

J	F	M	A	M	J
J	A	S	O	N	D

Cedar Elm
Ulmus crassifolia

ID FACT FILE

CROWN
Open, spreading

BARK
Pale brown,
furrowed, and
ridged

TWIGS
Brown, hairy,
sometimes
winged

LEAVES
Alternate, 1–2in,
in 2 rows, oval,
toothed,
leathery, dark
green above,
paler and hairy
below, turning
yellow in autumn

FLOWERS
Appearing before
the leaves, tiny,
greenish, without
petals, in
clusters

FRUITS
Up to ⅜in,
elliptical,
flattened, green,
whitish-hairy,
with a narrow
wing

Cedar Elm is a common tree where it is found, although it has a fairly restricted distribution, from western Tennessee and Mississippi, west to Texas and Mexico. A further, isolated population is also known from northern Florida. It is usually found on limestone soils and while also susceptible to Dutch Elm disease, it is not so badly affected as the related American Elm (*U. americana*).

ELM FAMILY, ULMACEAE

Deciduous
Up to 70ft

J	F	M	A	M	J
J	A	S	O	N	D

Slippery Elm
Ulmus rubra

ID FACT FILE

CROWN
Open, spreading

BARK
Dark brown,
deeply furrowed,
inner bark gum-
like and slippery

TWIGS
Brown, hairy,
sometimes
winged

LEAVES
Alternate, 5–7in,
in 2 rows,
elliptical, toothed,
leathery, dark
green and rough
above, paler and
softly hairy below,
turning yellow in
autumn

FLOWERS
Appearing before
the leaves, tiny,
greenish, without
petals, in clusters

FRUITS
Up to ¾in,
rounded,
flattened, green,
hairy not ciliate,
with a broad wing

Slippery Elm is so named for the edible
mucilaginous inner bark, which is
characteristic for this species. This bark was
also formerly used medicinally. Unfortunately,
like other species of elm, it is susceptible to
disease. Despite this tendency it is
nevertheless occasionally seen as an
ornamental tree. It is naturally found east of a
line from the eastern Dakotas to eastern Texas
but is uncommon along the Gulf Coast and
only found in the north of Florida.

WALNUT FAMILY, JUGLANDACEAE

Deciduous
Up to 100ft

J	F	M	A	M	J
J	A	S	O	N	D

Water Hickory
Carya aquatica

ID FACT FILE

CROWN
Narrow

BARK
Brown, smooth, becoming fissured and scaly

TWIGS
Brown, slender, hairy when young

LEAVES
Alternate, pinnate, leaflets 9–13, lance-shaped, toothed, up to 5in, dark green, hairy below

FLOWERS
Appearing before the leaves, greenish, males in usually 3 drooping catkins up to 3in, females tiny at tips of same stalks

FRUITS
¾–1½in, elliptical, flattened, husk brown, with 4 wings, seeds many

This tree is the largest of the hickories and, as its name suggests, is a constituent of wetland habitats and can cope with sites that may become submerged at intervals. Unlike other species of the same genus, it is generally of no commercial value either for its wood or for its bitter nuts, although they are consumed by aquatic wildlife. It is naturally found in Virginia, south to Florida, and west to Texas; some populations range north to Illinois.

WALNUT FAMILY, JUGLANDACEAE

Deciduous
Up to 80ft

J	F	M	A	M	J
J	A	S	O	N	D

Bitternut Hickory
Carya cordiformis

ID FACT FILE

CROWN
Broad, rounded

BARK
Gray to pale
brown, shallowly
furrowed

TWIGS
Slender,
terminating in
bright yellow buds

LEAVES
Alternate,
pinnate, leaflets
7–9, lance-
shaped, toothed,
up to 6in, pale
green, hairy
below, turning
yellow in autumn

FLOWERS
Appearing before
the leaves,
greenish, males
in drooping
catkins up to
3in, females tiny
at tips of same
stalks

FRUITS
1in, rounded or
pear-shaped,
husk green, with
4 wings, seeds
many, gray,
smooth

This species, the most common and widespread
of the hickories, is found throughout the eastern
states at low elevations in mixed hardwood
forests, as far west as Minnesota to Texas. Easily
recognizable by its yellow winter buds, this tree
is little foraged but has some commercial use as
a timber tree and in the smoking of meat.

WALNUT FAMILY, JUGLANDACEAE

Deciduous
Up to 80ft

J	F	M	A	M	J
J	A	S	O	N	D

Pignut
Carya glabra

ID FACT FILE

CROWN
Irregular,
spreading

BARK
Gray, shallowly
furrowed

TWIGS
Slender, brown,
hairless

LEAVES
Alternate,
pinnate, leaflets
usually 5, lance-
shaped, toothed,
up to 6in, pale
green, sometimes
hairy below,
turning yellow
in autumn

FLOWERS
Appearing before
the leaves,
greenish, males
in drooping
catkins up to
3in, females tiny
at tips of same
stalks

FRUITS
1–2in, rounded
or pear-shaped,
husk green
becoming brown,
splitting in the
middle, revealing
thick-walled nut
containing small
bittersweet seed

Although not as widespread as Bitternut
Hickory, this species is found from Maine south
to Florida and west as far as Iowa and Texas;
it is abundant in some areas,
such as the Appalachian
Mountains. Unlike its relative,
the palatable nut is valued
both by local wildlife and
humans, and the wood is also
widely used for its strength and
elasticity.

WALNUT FAMILY, JUGLANDACEAE

Deciduous
Up to 100ft

J	F	M	A	M	J
J	A	S	O	N	D

Pecan
Carya illinoinensis

ID FACT FILE

CROWN
Broad, rounded

BARK
Gray-brown,
irregularly
furrowed

TWIGS
Pale gray-brown,
smooth

LEAVES
Alternate,
pinnate, leaflets
11–17, narrowly
lance-shaped,
curved, toothed,
up to 7in, yellow-
green above,
paler below,
turning yellow in
autumn

FLOWERS
Appearing before
the leaves,
greenish, males
in usually 3
drooping catkins
up to 3in,
females tiny at
tips of same
stalks

FRUITS
1–2in, oblong,
husk brown, with
4 wings, nuts
thin-shelled
containing edible
seed

Pecan is native to Iowa across to southern Indiana and south through the Mississippi valley to Louisiana and west to Texas, Oklahoma, and Kansas, although largely absent from the Ozark Plateau. However, the natural range may have previously been extended through cultivation. Today it is one of the most important economic trees of North America and is widely cultivated outside of its natural range for its wood, but mostly for the edible nuts, which it produces in huge quantities once established.

WALNUT FAMILY, JUGLANDACEAE

Deciduous
Up to 100ft

J	F	M	A	M	J
J	A	S	O	N	D

Shellbark Hickory

Carya laciniosa

ID FACT FILE

CROWN
Narrowly rounded

BARK
Gray, peeling in
loose strips

TWIGS
Orange, hairy,
ending in large
hairy bud

LEAVES
Alternate,
pinnate, leaflets
usually 7, lance-
shaped, toothed,
up to 8in, shiny
green above,
paler and hairy
below, turning
bronze in autumn

FLOWERS
Appearing before
the leaves,
greenish, males
in usually 3
drooping catkins
up to 3in,
females tiny at
tips of same
stalks

FRUITS
1½–2½in,
rounded,
flattened, husk
brown, with 4
wings splitting
to base, nuts
thick-shelled
containing edible
seed

A large but economically unimportant species of hickory, this is a relatively uncommon species with a very scattered distribution from Pennsylvania and Ohio in the north, and southwest to Tennessee and Oklahoma. Isolated populations are also found in New York, Georgia, and Mississippi. The nuts are thick-shelled and generally not harvested or foraged, although many cultivars exist in an attempt to interbreed the species with Pecan, to improve the quality of the nuts of that species.

WALNUT FAMILY, JUGLANDACEAE

Deciduous
Up to 80ft

J	F	M	A	M	J
J	A	S	O	N	D

Nutmeg Hickory
Carya myristiciformis

ID FACT FILE

CROWN
Open, spreading

BARK
Gray, becoming
fissured

TWIGS
Brown, slender,
with small brown
or yellow scales

LEAVES
Alternate,
pinnate, leaflets
5–9, lance-
shaped, toothed,
up to 5in, green
and hairy above,
shiny and whitish
below, turning
bronze in autumn

FLOWERS
Appearing before
the leaves,
greenish, males
in usually 3
drooping catkins
up to 3in,
females tiny at
tips of same
stalks

FRUITS
¾–1½in,
elliptical, husk
yellow-brown,
hairy, with 4
wings splitting
to base, nuts
thick-shelled
containing edible
seed

Nutmeg Hickory is so named for the likeness to the nut that produces nutmeg. It is an uncommon species with a scattered and localized distribution from South Carolina, west to Alabama, Mississippi, Louisiana, and Texas, and north to Arkansas. Often found in association with Bastard Oak (*Quercus sinuata*), it is thought both species may represent relict populations of a previously more widespread flora.

WALNUT FAMILY, JUGLANDACEAE

Deciduous
Up to 100ft

J	F	M	A	M	J
J	A	S	O	N	D

Shagbark Hickory
Carya ovata

ID FACT FILE

CROWN
Narrow, irregular

BARK
Gray, semi-peeling in long curved strips remaining attached in the middle

TWIGS
Brown, smooth, terminating in hairy buds with spiny scales

LEAVES
Alternate, pinnate, leaflets 5–7, elliptical, toothed, up to 7in, yellow-green above, paler below, turning bronze in autumn

FLOWERS
Appearing before the leaves, greenish, males in drooping catkins up to 3in, females tiny

FRUITS
1¼–2½in, rounded, husk brown, with 4 thick wings splitting to middle, nuts rounded and flattened, containing edible seed

This species is probably the most important of the hickories along with Pecan. It has an extensive range throughout the eastern states and is found as far west as Minnesota south to Texas although it is not seen in the extreme southeastern Gulf states. Shagbark Hickory is the source of commercial hickory nuts, which are also attractive to wildlife, and the wood is also highly valued for a range of uses.

WALNUT FAMILY, JUGLANDACEAE

Deciduous
Up to 30ft

J	F	M	A	M	J
J	A	S	O	N	D

Black Hickory
Carya texana

ID FACT FILE

CROWN
Irregular,
spreading

BARK
Dark gray, deeply
fissured

TWIGS
Brown, hairy
when young

LEAVES
Alternate,
pinnate, leaflets
usually 7, lance-
shaped, toothed,
up to 6in, shiny
green above,
paler and hairy
below

FLOWERS
Appearing before
the leaves,
greenish, males
in usually 3
drooping catkins
up to 3in,
females tiny at
tips of same
stalks

FRUITS
¾–1½in, rounded,
husk brown, with
4 unpronounced
wings splitting
to base, nuts
thick-shelled
containing edible
or sometimes
bitter seed

The westernmost hickory species found in
North America, Black Hickory ranges west of
the Mississippi River from southern Indiana as
far southwest as south-central Texas. It is most
commonly seen as a component
of oak woodland on dry,
rocky or sandy uplands.
It is occasionally grown as an
ornamental tree but otherwise is
of little commercial importance
due to its relative small size.

WALNUT FAMILY, JUGLANDACEAE

Deciduous
Up to 80ft

J	F	M	A	M	J
J	A	S	O	N	D

Mockernut
Carya tomentosa

ID FACT FILE

CROWN
Narrow to rounded, open

BARK
Gray, irregularly furrowed

TWIGS
Brown, densely hairy terminating in hairy buds

LEAVES
Alternate, pinnate, leaflets 7–9, elliptical, toothed, up to 8in, yellow-green above, paler and densely hairy below, turning yellow in autumn, aromatic

FLOWERS
Appearing before the leaves, greenish, males in drooping catkins up to 3in, females tiny

FRUITS
1½–2in, elliptical, husk brown, with 4 wings splitting almost to base, nuts rounded, thick-shelled, containing edible seed

This large, wide-ranging tree is found from Texas north to Iowa and all states east except the Great Lakes region and southern Florida. Although the nuts produced are edible and highly attractive to wildlife, they are not so commonly consumed by people because of their thick shells. However, the wood is highly valued and used for tools and furniture and as with many other hickories, charcoal produced from the wood is widely used for smoking meats.

WALNUT FAMILY, JUGLANDACEAE

Deciduous
Up to 80ft

| J | F | M | A | M | J |
| J | A | S | O | N | D |

Butternut
Juglans cinerea

ID FACT FILE

CROWN
Open, broad

BARK
Gray, becoming
furrowed

TWIGS
Brown, with
sticky hairs

LEAVES
Alternate,
pinnate with
11–17 leaflets
each 2–4in long,
aromatic, yellow-
green above,
paler and softly
hairy below,
turning yellow in
autumn

FLOWERS
Small, greenish,
males in catkins,
pendent, 2–4in,
females in
clusters of 6–8
at tips of same
twig

FRUITS
1½–2½in, egg-
shaped in
clusters, husk
fleshy with rust-
colored hairs,
containing
wrinkled, brown
nut

An uncommon but widely distributed species native to the northeastern states as far west as Missouri and Minnesota, and as far south as Georgia. Relatively short-lived and only occasionally seen as an ornamental tree, and having soft wood, it is nonetheless valued for its edible nuts, which are also highly prized by wildlife. Oil from the nut is also harvested and the husk is the source of an orange or yellow dye.

WALNUT FAMILY, JUGLANDACEAE

Deciduous
Up to 100ft

J	F	M	A	M	J
J	A	S	O	N	D

Black Walnut
Juglans nigra

ID FACT FILE

CROWN
Open, rounded

BARK
Dark brown,
becoming
furrowed into
ridges

TWIGS
Brown, stout

LEAVES
Alternate,
pinnate with
9–21 leaflets
each 2½–5in
long, aromatic,
dark green, hairy
below, turning
yellow in autumn

FLOWERS
Small, greenish,
males in catkins,
pendent, 3–5in,
females in
clusters of 2–5
at tips of same
twig

FRUITS
1½–2½in, egg-
shaped in
clusters, husk
fleshy, green to
brown, containing
wrinkled, brown
nut

Found in isolated localized populations throughout the eastern states except in the north and absent from the Mississippi delta, Black Walnut is a highly valued tree ranging east of a line from South Dakota to Texas. The wood is strong and resilient and much used in furniture and cabinet making. The edible nuts, a source of food for local mammals, are also harvested commercially in plantations. It is sometimes also grown ornamentally.

WALNUT FAMILY, JUGLANDACEAE

Deciduous
Up to 30ft

| J | F | M | A | M | J |
| J | A | S | O | N | D |

Little Walnut
Juglans microcarpa

ID FACT FILE

CROWN
Broad, rounded

BARK
Gray, darkening with age and becoming furrowed

TWIGS
Greenish-brown, with brownish hairy buds

LEAVES
Alternate, pinnate with 7–13 (or more) leaflets each 2–3in long, finely toothed, aromatic, yellow-green above, paler below, turning yellow in autumn

FLOWERS
Small, greenish, males in catkins, pendent, 2–4in, females in clusters of 6–8 at tips of same twig

FRUITS
½–¾in, egg-shaped in clusters, husk thin with rust-colored hairs, containing wrinkled, brown nut

This walnut is native to the southern central states of Kansas, New Mexico, and Texas, where it is found growing in rocky streambeds and valleys, and on low foothills. The common name derives from the characteristically small nuts, which are only ⅜in in diameter at their largest. They are an important food source for many small animals. In common with other walnuts, this species produces chemicals to inhibit the growth of other competitive species and the wood is also used as a veneer.

BEECH FAMILY, FAGACEAE

Deciduous
Up to 100ft

J	F	M	A	M	J
J	A	S	O	N	D

American Chestnut
Castanea dentata

ID FACT FILE

CROWN
Broadly rounded

BARK
Gray-brown, smooth on sprouts, becoming furrowed on older specimens unaffected by blight

TWIGS
Green, hairless

LEAVES
Alternate, elliptical, toothed, pointed at apex, up to 9in, shiny yellow-green above, paler below, turning yellow in autumn

FLOWERS
Tiny, males in erect catkins up to 8in, females tiny, at base of male catkins

FRUITS
2–2½in, a bur, husk spiny, nuts 2–3, shiny-brown, edible

Previously an important commercial tree valued both for the durable wood and for the edible nuts it produces. However, the occurrence of chestnut blight early in the last century has decimated the wild population of this species. All trees within the natural range are killed although they will resprout from the roots, albeit producing much smaller specimens. Cultivated trees outside the natural range (from Maine south to Georgia and west to Mississippi and Indiana) are, however, unaffected. The species was also formerly exploited for tannins produced from the bark, and a variety of medicinal products were also derived from the tree.

BEECH FAMILY, FAGACEAE

Deciduous
Up to 40ft

J	F	M	A	M	J
J	A	S	O	N	D

Allegheny Chinkapin
Castanea pumila

This small tree with a short trunk is sometimes shrublike and thicket-forming. It is found in upland woods associating with hickory and oak species in the southeast of the United States roughly east of a line from New Jersey to east Texas, and although widespread it is not particularly common. It will readily hybridize with both American Chestnut (*C. dentata*) and Ozark Chinkapin (*C. ozarkensis*) where the species are found together.

ID FACT FILE

CROWN
Broadly rounded

BARK
Reddish-brown, furrowed

TWIGS
Gray, hairy when young

LEAVES
Alternate, elliptical, toothed, pointed at apex, up to 6in, yellow-green above, paler and hairy below

FLOWERS
Tiny, males in erect catkins up to 6in, females tiny, at base of male catkins

FRUITS
1in, a bur, husk spiny, nuts single, brown, edible

BEECH FAMILY, FAGACEAE

Deciduous
Up to 80ft

J	F	M	A	M	J
J	A	S	O	N	D

American Beech
Fagus grandiflora

ID FACT FILE

CROWN
Rounded, spreading

BARK
Gray, smooth

TWIGS
Reddish-brown, slender, spurred, terminating in long, scaly, sharp-pointed buds

LEAVES
Alternate, 2½–5in, elliptical, finely toothed, shiny, pointed at apex, dark green above, paler below, turning bronze in autumn

FLOWERS
Tiny, males in ball-like clusters at tips of shoots, females paired

FRUITS
Up to ¾in, husk prickly, 4-lobed, containing 2 small triangular nuts, shiny brown, edible

American Beech is a long-lived stately tree found throughout the eastern states east of a line from Michigan to Texas, except in southern Florida. It inhabits a wide variety of habitats, although is usually found as a canopy tree in deciduous woodlands on acidic soils. It may also be seen in pure stands. Generally growing at higher elevations in the south of its range, it is widely grown as a landscape tree for its form and autumn color. The nuts are edible and widely consumed both by people and animals.

BEECH FAMILY, FAGACEAE

Deciduous
Up to 100ft

| J | F | M | A | M | J |
| J | A | S | O | N | D |

White Oak
Quercus alba

ID FACT FILE

CROWN
Rounded, spreading

BARK
Pale gray, shallowly fissured forming ridges or scaly plates

TWIGS
Reddish-brown, slender, with rounded buds

LEAVES
Alternate, 4–9in, elliptical, shallowly 5–9-lobed, slightly toothed, green above, whitish below

FLOWERS
Usually appearing with the leaves, tiny, inconspicuous, without petals, males in pendulous clusters, females solitary or in small clusters, males and females in separate clusters

FRUITS
Acorn to 1¼in, egg-shaped, cup shallow, quarter the length of acorn, scales becoming warty and hairy, gray

A fairly long-lived (up to 600 years) tree, the White Oak had been an important timber tree since Colonial times, when it was used extensively in shipbuilding. Today, its major use is in the construction of whiskey barrels, furniture, and flooring, and as a stately ornamental tree for its reddish-brown autumn color. It is found all over the eastern states as far south as northern Florida and as far west as Texas in the south and Minnesota in the north.

BEECH FAMILY, FAGACEAE

Deciduous
Up to 70ft

J	F	M	A	M	J
J	A	S	O	N	D

Swamp White Oak
Quercus bicolor

ID FACT FILE

CROWN
Rounded to irregular

BARK
Pale gray, becoming furrowed into large plates

TWIGS
Pale brown, with blunt buds at the tip

LEAVES
Alternate, 4–7in, obovate, irregularly lobed, lobes shallow, shiny green above, paler and hairy below,

FLOWERS
Usually appearing with the leaves, tiny, inconspicuous, without petals, males in pendulous clusters, females solitary or in small clusters, males and females in separate clusters

FRUITS
Acorn to 1¼in, egg-shaped, cup deep, third the length of acorn, scales prominent, brown

As the common name suggests, *Q. bicolor* is a wetland species found alongside rivers, lakes, and swamps, more or less east of a line from Minnesota to Missouri. It tends to be found in localized, isolated populations in North Carolina, Tennessee, and Kansas. It is an important tree in the wild in terms of preventing erosion of wetland habitats, and also as a food source for a variety of animals. The durable wood is used in furniture and boatbuilding.

BEECH FAMILY, FAGACEAE

Deciduous
Up to 80ft

J	F	M	A	M	J
J	A	S	O	N	D

Scarlet Oak
Quercus coccinea

ID FACT FILE

CROWN
Rounded, open

BARK
Gray, smooth, becoming black-ish and thickly furrowed into plates or ridges

TWIGS
Reddish-brown, slender, with rounded buds

LEAVES
Alternate, 4–6in, elliptical, deeply 7–9-lobed, each lobe bristle-toothed at tip, shiny green above, paler below, turning scarlet in autumn

FLOWERS
Usually appear-ing with the leaves, tiny, inconspicuous, without petals, males in pendu-lous clusters, females solitary or in small clusters

FRUITS
Acorn to 1in, egg-shaped, cup half the length of acorn, scales tightly pressed, becoming brown with faint rings, maturing in second year

Popular as a landscape or ornamental tree on account of the brilliant scarlet autumn color, Scarlet Oak is also harvested to some degree for its timber (which is usually sold as Red Oak, a related species). Found in mixed hardwood forests on upland ridges, the species naturally ranges from Maine and Indiana in the north, south to Louisiana and Georgia.

BEECH FAMILY, FAGACEAE

Deciduous
Up to 80ft

J	F	M	A	M	J
J	A	S	O	N	D

Southern Red Oak
Quercus falcata

ID FACT FILE

CROWN
Rounded, open

BARK
Gray, furrowed into plates or ridges

TWIGS
Slender, with rounded buds at the tip

LEAVES
Alternate, 4–8in, elliptical, deeply 1–3-lobed with elongated lobe at tip, lobes bristle-toothed at tip, shiny green above, paler and hairy below, turning brown in autumn

FLOWERS
Usually appearing with the leaves, tiny, inconspicuous, without petals, males in pendulous clusters, females solitary or in small clusters

FRUITS
Acorn to ⅝in, elliptical to rounded, cup third the length of acorn, scales becoming brown when mature in second year

Southern Red Oak is a valued tree, both for its timber and also as an ornamental tree for its attractive form. It is a relatively fast-growing but short-lived oak, living only for about 150 years. It is a native of mixed upland forests and is found from New Jersey south to Florida and west to Texas and Missouri. Like all oaks, it is an important food source in the form of the acorns, and also provides a valuable habitat for wildlife.

BEECH FAMILY, FAGACEAE

Deciduous
Up to 60ft

J	F	M	A	M	J
J	A	S	O	N	D

Shingle Oak
Quercus imbricaria

ID FACT FILE

CROWN
Conical, becoming rounded

BARK
Gray-brown, becoming furrowed and scaly

TWIGS
Greenish-brown, with pointed reddish-brown buds

LEAVES
Alternate, 4–8in, broadly lanceolate, with a bristle at the tip, shiny green above, paler and hairy below, turning yellow or brown in autumn

FLOWERS
Usually appearing with the leaves, tiny, inconspicuous, without petals, males in pendulous clusters, females solitary or in small clusters

FRUITS
Acorn to ⅝in, rounded, cup deep, third or half the length of acorn, scales hairy, brown, maturing in second year

Shingle Oak is a relatively common eastern oak often found in association with other oak species, particularly Post Oak (*Q. stellata*) and Black oak (*Q. velutina*). The main center of distribution ranges across the Great Plains from Arkansas in the south to Iowa and Michigan in the north, east to Pennsylvania extending southward to North Carolina. Isolated populations are also known from Louisiana and Alabama. It is best known for its use in the production of shingles. It is a very hardy but slow-growing tree that is able to tolerate quite cold temperatures, and it also transplants well, which makes it a popular semi-grown tree for ornamental plantings, such as in parks and streets.

BEECH FAMILY, FAGACEAE

Deciduous
Up to 40ft

| J | F | M | A | M | J |
| J | A | S | O | N | D |

Turkey Oak
Quercus laevis

ID FACT FILE

CROWN
Irregular, open

BARK
Gray-black, thick, furrowed into ridges

TWIGS
Slender, with rounded buds at the tip

LEAVES
Alternate, 4–8in, triangular, usually 3–5-lobed, each lobe bristle-toothed at tip, shiny yellow-green above, pale-green and hairy below

FLOWERS
Usually appearing with the leaves, tiny, inconspicuous, without petals, males in pendulous clusters, females solitary or in small clusters

FRUITS
Acorn to 1in, egg-shaped, cup third the length of acorn, scales hairy, becoming brown when mature in second year

Turkey Oak is a small tree adapted to habitats subjected to some fire disturbance, after which it frequently spreads by underground runners. It is found along the coastal plain from Virginia to central Florida westward to Louisiana. Being intolerant of salt spray, it is usually found near, rather than on the coast. The common name refers to the lobed leaves said to resemble turkey's feet.

BEECH FAMILY, FAGACEAE

Bur Oak
Quercus macrocarpa

ID FACT FILE

CROWN
Open, broad

BARK
Gray-black, deeply furrowed and ridged

TWIGS
Pale brown, often with corky ridges

LEAVES
Alternate, 5–10in, obovate, shallowly 5–9-lobed, lobes rounded, blue-green above, paler and variably hairy below

FLOWERS
Usually appearing with the leaves, tiny, inconspicuous, without petals, males in pendulous clusters, females solitary or in small clusters, males and females in separate clusters

FRUITS
Acorn to 2½in, broadly elliptical, cup deep and fringed, half the length of acorn, scales hairy, gray

A tree of the interior eastern states, found from Texas northeast to Pennsylvania and New York, and northwest from Texas to North Dakota, in prairie, savanna, and mixed woodlands. It is also widespread across southeast Canada and is the northernmost of the New World oak species, and also the species with the largest acorns. It is tolerant of pollution and consequently commonly planted as a street tree in urban areas.

BEECH FAMILY, FAGACEAE

Deciduous
Up to 50ft

J	F	M	A	M	J
J	A	S	O	N	D

Blackjack Oak
Quercus marilandica

ID FACT FILE

CROWN
Irregular

BARK
Very dark brown,
deeply furrowed
and ridged

TWIGS
Dark brown, hairy
when young, with
long reddish-
brown buds

LEAVES
Alternate,
2½–5in, obovate,
shallowly 3-
lobed, lobes
bristle-tipped,
shiny green
above, paler and
hairy below

FLOWERS
Usually
appearing with
the leaves, tiny,
inconspicuous,
without petals,
males in
pendulous
clusters, females
solitary or in
small clusters

FRUITS
Acorn to ¾in,
elliptical, ending
in a prominent
point, cup deep,
half the length of
acorn, scales
loose, hairy,
brown, maturing
in second year

A somewhat unattractive tree that is not utilized
as an ornamental species although it is wind-,
drought-, and salt-resistant. It tends to grow on
poor soils, where it may become the dominant
species, although on very poor soils, it
becomes shrubby. Originally
described more than 300 years
ago, it is found roughly east
of a line from Iowa to Texas
although it is absent from central
and southern Florida, and most
notably the Mississippi delta. The
timber has been used for railroad
ties, fencing, and charcoal.

BEECH FAMILY, FAGACEAE

Deciduous
Up to 80ft

J	F	M	A	M	J
J	A	S	O	N	D

Swamp Chestnut Oak
Quercus michauxii

ID FACT FILE

CROWN
Rounded

BARK
Gray, becoming furrowed and scaly

TWIGS
Orange-brown, often finely hairy, with pointed reddish-brown buds clustered at ends of twigs

LEAVES
Alternate, 4–9in, elliptical, pointed at tip, bluntly toothed, shiny green above, paler and hairy below, turning reddish-brown in autumn

FLOWERS
Usually appearing with the leaves, tiny, inconspicuous, without petals, males in pendulous clusters, females solitary or in small clusters

FRUITS
Acorn to 1¼in, egg-shaped, cup deep, third the length of acorn, scales brown, hairy

Swamp Chestnut Oak is an upland forest tree found in moist sites, usually alongside streams and swamp edges. It ranges along the coastal plain from Maryland south to Florida, as far east as eastern Texas, and north along the Mississippi and Ohio river valleys to Illinois and Indiana. Although not used ornamentally, the wood is widely used in flooring and splints of wood from this tree have been used for making baskets giving rise to an alternative common name, "Basket Oak."

Deciduous
Up to 80ft

J	F	M	A	M	J
J	A	S	O	N	D

Chinkapin Oak
Quercus muehlenbergii

ID FACT FILE

CROWN
Irregular

BARK
Pale gray,
fissured and
scaly

TWIGS
Brown, with
pointed buds
clustered at the
ends of twigs

LEAVES
Alternate, 5–8in,
elliptical,
coarsely toothed,
teeth gland-
tipped, shiny
green above,
paler below

FLOWERS
Usually
appearing with
the leaves, tiny,
inconspicuous,
without petals,
males in
pendulous
clusters, females
solitary or in
small clusters,
males and
females in
separate clusters

FRUITS
Acorn to 1¼in,
oval, cup deep,
third the length
of acorn, scales
ragged, hairy,
brown

A large, attractive tree, Chinkapin Oak is
widely distributed from Vermont to Wisconsin,
south through Iowa to Texas and New Mexico,
and east to Florida, but notably absent from
the Atlantic and Gulf coasts. It is usually
found on upland rocky limestone
soils, where it tends to dominate
along with other hardwood
species. It is a useful
ornamental tree where its
size can be accommodated,
and the wood is also used
for cabinet making and
furniture.

BEECH FAMILY, FAGACEAE

Water Oak
Quercus nigra

ID FACT FILE

CROWN
Conical or rounded

BARK
Dark gray, smooth, darkening and becoming fissured and ridged

TWIGS
Both twigs and pointed buds reddish-brown

LEAVES
Alternate, 2½–5in, variable, spathulate to obovate, tip sometimes 3-lobed, blue-green above, paler below

FLOWERS
Usually appearing with leaves, tiny, inconspicuous, without petals, males in pendulous clusters, females solitary or in small clusters

FRUITS
Acorn to ¾in, rounded, cup shallow, third the length of acorn, scales overlapping, brown, maturing in second year

Deciduous
Up to 100ft

J	F	M	A	M	J
J	A	S	O	N	D

Water Oak is found along the eastern coastal plains from New Jersey to Florida, and west to Texas, and ranging north along the Mississippi river to Missouri. It is a wetland species being found in floodplains, along rivers, and the edges of swamps. Consequently it is only occasionally grown as an ornamental tree on suitable soils, and the wood is not highly valued.

BEECH FAMILY, FAGACEAE

Deciduous
Up to 100ft

J	F	M	A	M	J
J	A	S	O	N	D

Pin Oak
Quercus palustris

ID FACT FILE

CROWN
Pyramidal

BARK
Dark gray, smooth becoming fissured

TWIGS
Slender, with rounded buds at the tip

LEAVES
Alternate, 3–5in, elliptical, usually 5–7-lobed, each lobe slightly toothed, shiny green above, pale-green and hairy below

FLOWERS
Usually appearing with the leaves, tiny, inconspicuous, without petals, males in pendulous clusters, females solitary or in small clusters

FRUITS
Acorn to ⅝in, rounded, cup third the length of acorn, scales thin, becoming brown when mature in second year

Found from New England south to North Carolina and west to Oklahoma and Iowa, Pin Oak is a native of moist upland and lowland soils and may be found in mixed forests or in pure stands. Although the timber is used in construction, its main importance is as an ornamental shade tree for which it is much used due to its attractive form and foliage, and fast growth.

BEECH FAMILY, FAGACEAE

Deciduous
Up to 80ft

J	F	M	A	M	J
J	A	S	O	N	D

Willow Oak
Quercus phellos

ID FACT FILE

CROWN
Rounded

BARK
Gray, smooth
becoming gray-
black and
fissured

TWIGS
Slender, with
rounded buds at
the tip

LEAVES
Alternate,
2–4½in, lance-
shaped, wavy-
edged with a
bristled tip,
green above,
pale-green and
sometimes hairy
below, turning
yellow in autumn

FLOWERS
Usually
appearing with
the leaves, tiny,
inconspicuous,
without petals,
males in
pendulous
clusters, females
solitary or in
small clusters

FRUITS
Acorn to ½in,
rounded, cup
quarter the length
of acorn, scales
becoming brown
when mature in
second year

A distinctive oak, easily recognized by the nonlobed, willowlike leaves, this species is shallow-rooted and easily transplanted and consequently, is commonly planted as an amenity tree. It is naturally found from New Jersey to northern Florida, east to Texas, and north along the Mississippi River to Illinois, where it usually occurs in lowland sites and floodplains (where it is tolerant of winter flooding).

BEECH FAMILY, FAGACEAE

Shumard Oak
Quercus shumardii

Deciduous
Up to 100ft

J	F	M	A	M	J
J	A	S	O	N	D

ID FACT FILE

CROWN
Open, rounded

BARK
Dark-gray,
smooth becoming
fissured

TWIGS
Slender, with
rounded brown
buds at the tip

LEAVES
Alternate, 3–7in,
elliptical, usually
5–9-lobed, each
lobe coarsely
toothed at tip,
shiny green and
hairy above, pale-
green and hairy
below, turning
red in autumn

FLOWERS
Usually appearing
with the leaves,
tiny, inconspic-
uous, without
petals, males in
pendulous
clusters, females
solitary or in
small clusters,
males and
females in
separate clusters

FRUITS
Acorn to 1in, egg-
shaped, cup third
the length of
acorn, scales
blunt, green,
becoming brown
when mature in
second year

Found from North Carolina south to Florida, and west to Kansas and central Texas, with local populations also found as far north as Pennsylvania and Michigan where, however, it is not so hardy. Shumard Oak is a native of moist sites and tolerant of poor soils, and is usually found along floodplains though also on dry ridge tops. It is often planted as a shade or ornamental tree.

BEECH FAMILY, FAGACEAE

Deciduous
Up to 120ft

J	F	M	A	M	J
J	A	S	O	N	D

Northern Red Oak
Quercus rubra

A widespread and common tree, Northern Red Oak is the northernmost of the eastern species, found from southeastern Canada into Maine and throughout the northeastern states as far south as Georgia and west to Oklahoma and Minnesota. It is also widely planted as an ornamental tree for its vivid red autumn color and is an important timber tree, used in a variety of ways but especially furniture and flooring.

ID FACT FILE

CROWN
Rounded, open

BARK
Gray, furrowed

TWIGS
Reddish, slender, with rounded buds at the tip

LEAVES
Alternate, 5–9in, elliptical, usually 7–11-lobed, each lobe bristle-toothed at tip, green above, pale-green and sometimes hairy below, turning dark red in autumn

FLOWERS
Usually appearing with the leaves, tiny, inconspicuous, without petals, males in pendulous clusters, females solitary or in small clusters

FRUITS
Acorn to 1in, egg-shaped, cup quarter the length of acorn, scales finely hairy, becoming reddish-brown when mature in second year

BEECH FAMILY, FAGACEAE

Deciduous
Up to 70ft

J	F	M	A	M	J
J	A	S	O	N	D

Post Oak
Quercus stellata

ID FACT FILE

CROWN
Rounded

BARK
Gray, becoming
deeply fissured
and ridged

TWIGS
Gray-brown,
densely hairy,
with many
lenticels, with
blunt orange-
brown buds at
ends of twigs

LEAVES
Alternate, 4–6in,
oblong, deeply
5–7-lobed, shiny
green above,
with scattered
star-shaped
hairs, paler
below, brown in
autumn

FLOWERS
Tiny,
inconspicuous,
without petals,
males in pendu-
lous clusters,
females solitary
or in small
clusters

FRUITS
Acorn to 1in,
elliptical, cup
half the length of
acorn, scales
green becoming
brown

Tolerant of drought, Post Oak is commonly found in mixed oak and pine forests on dry upland sites, ranging from Massachussets west to Iowa in the north, and south to Texas and Florida. An important habitat tree where it is found, both as a food source and for the cover it provides, it is also used commercially for a variety of construction purposes.

BEECH FAMILY, FAGACEAE

Deciduous
Up to 80ft

| J | F | M | A | M | J |
| J | A | S | O | N | D |

Black Oak
Quercus velutina

ID FACT FILE

CROWN
Open, spreading

BARK
Gray, smooth, becoming blackish and furrowed into ridges

TWIGS
Slender, with rounded buds at the tip

LEAVES
Alternate, 4–9in, elliptical, usually 7–9-lobed, each lobe bristle-toothed at tip, shiny green above, yellow-green and often hairy below

FLOWERS
Tiny, inconspicuous, without petals, males in pendulous clusters, females solitary or in small clusters

FRUITS
Acorn to ¾in, elliptical, cup half the length of acorn, scales hairy, becoming reddish-brown when mature in second year

Black Oak is a fairly widespread species on dry to moist upland slopes across the eastern states from Maine to northern Florida and westward to Texas, north to Minnesota. The wood is sold as Red Oak and used for furniture and flooring. Tannin was formerly extracted from the bark, and the yellow inner bark was a source of a yellow dye for clothing. It is an important tree for wildlife, both for the acorns and as a nesting site.

BEECH FAMILY, FAGACEAE

Evergreen
Up to 50ft

| J | F | M | A | M | J |
| J | A | S | O | N | D |

Live Oak
Quercus virginiana

ID FACT FILE

CROWN
Broad, rounded

BARK
Gray-brown,
deeply furrowed
and ridged

TWIGS
Gray, hairy, with
blunt buds
clustered at the
ends of the twigs

LEAVES
Alternate,
2½–5in, elliptical,
leathery, shiny
green above,
gray-green and
hairy below

FLOWERS
Usually
appearing with
the leaves, tiny,
inconspicuous,
without petals,
males in
pendulous
clusters, females
solitary or in
small clusters,
males and
females in
separate clusters

FRUITS
Acorn to 1in,
oblong, cup
deep, third the
length of acorn,
scales warty,
brown

A popular amenity tree where given adequate room to attain its full potential, Live Oak is a large attractive tree all year round with evergreen foliage. It is found along the coastal plain from Virginia to Florida, and west to Texas, with localized populations in Oklahoma and Mexico, with up to 3 varieties currently recognized. It is a durable tree, tolerant of a wide range of conditions and was once the major timber tree used for shipbuilding.

BIRCH FAMILY, BETULACEAE

Deciduous
Up to 20ft

J	F	M	A	M	J
J	A	S	O	N	D

Speckled Alder
Alnus incana

ID FACT FILE

CROWN
Irregular

BARK
Gray, smooth with conspicuous lenticels

TWIGS
Gray-brown, hairy when young

LEAVES
Alternate, 2–4in, elliptical, irregularly double-toothed, dull dark green above, pale gray-green with soft hairs below

FLOWERS
Appearing before the leaves, male catkins yellow, drooping, 1½–3in, females reddish, ovoid, ¼in

FRUITS
Woody, conelike, ½in on short stalks, enclosing rounded flat nutlets

A small tree (sometimes a shrub), Speckled Alder is widespread across Canada almost to Alaska, and found in the United States south to Virginia and west to Iowa at altitudes almost at the timber line. It is a short-lived species but not without benefits. Like all alders, its roots have nitrogen-fixing properties and it is also used in watershed management, as well as being an important forage tree for wildlife.

BIRCH FAMILY, BETULACEAE

Deciduous
Up to 30ft

J	F	M	A	M	J
J	A	S	O	N	D

Seaside Alder
Alnus maritima

ID FACT FILE

Crown
Rounded

Bark
Gray-brown,
smooth

Twigs
Slender, hairy
when young

Leaves
Alternate, 2–4in,
elliptical, double-
toothed, dark
green above,
pale green and
sometimes hairy
below

Flowers
Appearing in the
autumn, male
catkins yellow,
drooping,
1½–2½in,
females reddish,
ovoid, ¼in

Fruits
Woody, conelike,
⅜–¾in on short
stalks, enclosing
rounded flat
nutlets, maturing
in second year

Named for its common habitat, Seaside Alder is a coastal species found on the eastern shores of Maryland and in wet places in Delaware. It is usually found in general proximity to coastline areas, but does not occur on the actual coast itself. The species has a disjunct distribution with an isolated range also in Oklahoma, where it is found at higher elevations than on the coast. Unusually among the Alders, it is an autumn-flowering species.

BIRCH FAMILY, BETULACEAE

Deciduous
Up to 80ft

J	F	M	A	M	J
J	A	S	O	N	D

Yellow Birch
Betula alleghaniensis

ID FACT FILE

CROWN
Broadly rounded

BARK
Yellowish to
silver-gray, shiny,
peeling in strips,
becoming
reddish-brown
and fissured with
age

TWIGS
Brown, slender,
hairy

LEAVES
Alternate,
3–5½in, elliptical,
double-toothed,
dull green above,
pale green
below, turning
yellow in autumn

FLOWERS
Tiny, males
yellowish in
drooping catkins
up to 4in,
females greenish
in erect catkins
up to 1½in, in
separate clusters
on the same twig

FRUIT
Conelike,
brownish up to
1¾in, hairy, with
many tiny winged
nutlets

Yellow Birch is an important commercial tree found in the northeast from Maine through the Great Lakes region to Minnesota and south along the Appalachians into Georgia. The timber of this large tree is widely used in furniture and cabinet-making and other parts of the tree are also used—the sap for a syrup and also the bark and leaves for making infusions. As with other birches, it is also an important tree for wildlife.

BIRCH FAMILY, BETULACEAE

Deciduous
Up to 80ft

J	F	M	A	M	J
J	A	S	O	N	D

Cherry Birch
Betula lenta

ID FACT FILE

CROWN
Rounded

BARK
Brown, smooth
with horizontal
lenticels, shiny,
becoming
fissured into
scaly plates

TWIGS
Brown, slender,
hairy

LEAVES
Alternate,
3–5½in, elliptical,
pointed at apex,
double-toothed,
dull green above,
pale yellow-green
below, turning
yellow in autumn

FLOWERS
Tiny, males
yellowish in
drooping catkins
up to 4in,
females greenish
in erect catkins
up to 1½in, in
separate clusters
on the same twig

FRUIT
Conelike,
brownish up to
1½in, with many
tiny winged
nutlets

Cherry Birch was previously a commercial source for Oil of Wintergreen and the aromatic twigs and foliage give off this odor when crushed. The bark, like that of the Yellow Birch, can also be tapped for the syrupy sap, which in turn when fermented, produces birch beer. The wood also has similar uses to this related species. A tree of the extreme northeast, its natural range is from Maine southwest through the Appalachians to Alabama and it is also found west to Ohio in the north of its range.

BIRCH FAMILY, BETULACEAE

Deciduous
Up to 80ft

| J | F | M | A | M | J |
| J | A | S | O | N | D |

River Birch
Betula nigra

ID FACT FILE

CROWN
Spreading

BARK
Gray to pinkish-brown, shiny, peeling in thin strips, becoming thickly fissured

TWIGS
Brown, slender, hairy

LEAVES
Alternate, 1½–3in, ovate, double-toothed, shiny green above, whitish and often hairy below, turning yellow in autumn

FLOWERS
Tiny, males yellowish in drooping catkins up to 4in, females greenish in erect catkins up to 1½in, in separate clusters on the same twig

FRUIT
Conelike, brownish up to 1½in, hairy, with many tiny winged nutlets

This moisture-loving tree is the southernmost birch representative in the United States. Although the timber of this tree is of limited value, its success in wetland habitats makes it an important species for soil stabilization. It is also of some importance for local wildlife and to some extent, is also grown ornamentally for its attractive bark. It is naturally found alongside rivers and lakes or in floodplains. The range is from Connecticut to Florida, westward to Texas from where it extends northward, just reaching into the state of Minnesota. It is not found in the Great Lakes region.

BIRCH FAMILY, BETULACEAE

Deciduous
Up to 90ft

J	F	M	A	M	J
J	A	S	O	N	D

Paper Birch
Betula papyrifera

Found at altitudes up to 4,000ft across the United States from New York and North Carolina to Oregon and Colorado, Paper Birch has a long history of human association. The peeling bark was previously used in the construction of canoes and the wood is a valuable timber. It also plays an important ecological role, being a food source for various woodland mammals and birds.

ID FACT FILE

CROWN
Erect, becoming open and spreading

BARK
White, peeling off in papery strips to reveal orange inner bark, with horizontal gray lenticels

TWIGS
Reddish-brown

LEAVES
Alternate, 1½–4in, oval, pointed at apex, double-toothed, dull green above, pale green below, turning yellow in autumn

FLOWERS
Tiny, males yellowish in drooping catkins up to 4in, females greenish in erect catkins up to 1½in, in separate clusters on the same twig

FRUIT
Conelike, brownish up to 2in, with many tiny winged nutlets

BIRCH FAMILY, BETULACEAE

Deciduous
Up to 40ft

J	F	M	A	M	J
J	A	S	O	N	D

American Hornbeam
Carpinus caroliniana

ID FACT FILE

CROWN
Broadly rounded, spreading

BARK
Gray, smooth

TWIGS
Brown, slender

LEAVES
Alternate, 2–4in, elliptical, pointed at apex, double-toothed, blue-green above, paler and hairy below, turning orange in autumn

FLOWERS
Appearing before the leaves, tiny, males greenish in drooping catkins up to 1½in, females reddish in pairs, catkins up to ¾in, in separate clusters

FRUIT
Up to ¼in, winged nutlets in pairs, green, hairy, with 3-lobed leafy bract, aggregated into drooping clusters up to 4in

American Hornbeam is an extremely widespread species found throughout the eastern states as far west as Texas and Minnesota in the north, although it is absent from the north of Maine and southern Florida. An understory component of hardwood forests, it is also found in Canada and Mexico. The wood is dense and strong but due to the small size of the tree, it is not of major commercial importance—being limited to the construction of small utensils and tools.

BIRCH FAMILY, BETULACEAE

Eastern Hophornbeam
Ostrya virginiana

Deciduous
Up to 50ft

J	F	M	A	M	J
J	A	S	O	N	D

ID FACT FILE

CROWN
Conical, becoming rounded

BARK
Gray-brown, fissured and scaly, peeling

TWIGS
Reddish-brown, smooth

LEAVES
Alternate, 2½–5in, oval, toothed, yellow-green above, paler and often hairy below, turning yellow in autumn

FLOWERS
Appearing before the leaves, tiny, inconspicuous, greenish, males in pendant catkins, usually in 3's, forming over winter, females in smaller catkins at the ends of twigs

FRUITS
Up to 2in, oval, conelike clusters of small nutlets, brown, papery

Eastern Hophornbeam is widespread across eastern North America, ranging from Manitoba to Nova Scotia in Canada, and south to Florida and Texas, although it becomes more scattered in the south of its range. It is very tolerant of shade and as such commonly grows as an understory tree in mixed hardwood forests. The wood is dense and hard and somewhat used, and this species is also often grown ornamentally as a small shade tree.

TEA FAMILY, THEACEAE

Evergreen
Up to 65ft

Loblolly Bay
Gordonia lasianthus

ID FACT FILE

CROWN
Columnar

BARK
Reddish-brown,
thickly furrowed

TWIGS
Brown, hairless

LEAVES
Alternate,
lanceolate to
elliptic, 4–6in,
leathery, toothed,
shiny green,
turning red
before falling,
throughout the
year

FLOWERS
Cup-shaped, up
to 2½in across,
5 large white
petals, with
many yellow
stamens,
solitary, fragrant

FRUITS
Up to ½in, gray,
hard, oval
capsule, hairy

The only New World representative of an
Asian genus, Loblolly Bay is a very attractive
tree with glossy-green evergreen foliage and
large cup-shaped white and yellow flowers.
Consequently it is often grown as an
ornamental tree for year-round interest.
Naturally, it is found in swamps and other wet
sites along the Atlantic coastal plain from
North Carolina to central Florida, and west
along the Gulf Coast to Mississippi.

LIME FAMILY, TILIACEAE

Deciduous
Up to 100ft

| J | F | M | A | M | J |
| J | A | S | O | N | D |

American Basswood
Tilia americana

ID FACT FILE

CROWN
Conical, dense, branches drooping at tips

BARK
Gray-brown, smooth becoming furrowed

TWIGS
Reddish-brown, slender, hairless

LEAVES
Alternate, 3–6in, heart-shaped, pointed at tip, toothed. Dark green above, paler below, turning yellow or brown in autumn

FLOWERS
Up to ⅝in, pale yellow in pendent clusters, with large green bract

FRUITS
Up to ½in, elliptical, nutlike, gray, hairy

American Basswood is usually found with other deciduous hardwoods in its native range in the northeast of America. It ranges from Maine south to North Carolina and as far west as Oklahoma and Minnesota in the United States, although it also occurs in Canada. Two varieties (var. *caroliniana* and var. *heterophylla*, which are sometimes recognized as distinct species) extend the range southward to Florida and Missouri. The wood is used for a variety of purposes and the species also makes an attractive ornamental specimen in parks or as a street tree, although it will not tolerate excessive pollution in an urban setting. Bees are very attracted to the flowers, producing a quality honey.

WILLOW FAMILY, SALICACEAE

Deciduous
Up to 80ft

| J | F | M | A | M | J |
| J | A | S | O | N | D |

White Poplar
Populus alba

ID FACT FILE

CROWN
Narrow, open

BARK
Gray, smooth, becoming furrowed with age

TWIGS
Brown, whitish-hairy when young

LEAVES
Alternate, 2–4in, oval, 3–5 lobed, gray-green above, densely whitish-hairy below, turning yellow or sometimes reddish in autumn

FLOWERS
Catkins up to 2½in, whitish-hairy, pendulous, males and females on separate trees

FRUITS
Up to ¼in, elliptical capsule, brown, splitting in 2 to release tiny cottony seeds

A distinctive poplar due to the characteristic leaves (white on the underside), *Populus alba* is originally native to southern Europe and Asia but was introduced to North America during Colonial times. It is widely grown and has become naturalized across much of the United States and southern Canada. It is an attractive and fast-growing ornamental tree, although its suckering habit can lead to it spreading to such an extent that it may become locally invasive.

WILLOW FAMILY, SALICACEAE

Deciduous
Up to 100ft

J	F	M	A	M	J
J	A	S	O	N	D

Balsam Poplar
Populus balsamifera

ID FACT FILE

CROWN
Narrow

BARK
Brown, smooth, becoming gray and furrowed into ridges

TWIGS
Brown, with sticky buds producing a yellow resin

LEAVES
Alternate, 3–5in, oval, pointed at tip, dark green above, paler below, hairless

FLOWERS
Catkins up to 4in, brown, pendulous, males and females on separate trees

FRUITS
Up to ½in, egg-shaped capsule, pointed at tip, brown, splitting in 2 to release tiny cottony seeds

One of the northernmost poplar species, this tree is found across the entire width of North America. In the United States it is found as far south as Pennsylvania and Iowa (with isolated localized populations also found in Virginia) and as far west as Colorado, although a subspecies (*Populus balsamifera* ssp. *trichocarpa*) is found in the extreme west from Alaska south to California and Utah. It is usually found alongside streams and lakes and is of some use in habitat stabilization in appropriate soil conditions.

WILLOW FAMILY, SALICACEAE

Deciduous
Up to 100ft

J	F	M	A	M	J
J	A	S	O	N	D

Eastern Cottonwood
Populus deltoides

ID FACT FILE

CROWN
Open, spreading

BARK
Yellow-green,
smooth,
becoming gray
and thickly
furrowed into
ridges

TWIGS
Brown, with
sticky buds

LEAVES
Alternate, 3–5in,
triangular,
pointed at tip,
coarsely toothed,
green, turning
yellow in autumn

FLOWERS
Catkins up to
4in, brown,
pendulous,
males and
females on
separate trees

FRUITS
Up to ½in,
elliptical capsule,
brown, splitting
in 3 or 4 to
release tiny
cottony seeds

Found throughout the Great Lakes area and the eastern states as far south as Texas and northern Florida. A western variety (var. *occidentalis*) is also known in Montana. Common along stream banks and other riparian habitats where it often acts as a pioneer tree. The wood is poor quality but is used as pulpwood and for making boxes and crates. Eastern Cottonwood is also widely planted across the plains as a shelterbelt tree.

WILLOW FAMILY, SALICACEAE

Deciduous
Up to 60ft

| J | F | M | A | M | J |
| J | A | S | O | N | D |

Bigtooth Aspen
Populus grandidentata

ID FACT FILE

CROWN
Narrow, open

BARK
Gray, smooth, darkening and becoming furrowed with age

TWIGS
Brown, hairy when young

LEAVES
Alternate, 2–4in, oval, pointed at tip, coarsely toothed, hairy when young, pale green, turning yellow in autumn

FLOWERS
Catkins up to 2½in, reddish-brown, pendulous, males and females on separate trees

FRUITS
Up to ¼in, elliptical capsule, brown, splitting in 2 to release tiny cottony seeds

A fast-growing colonizing species, Bigtooth Aspen is native to the northeast of the United States from Maine south to Virginia, across to Missouri and Minnesota, and is also found across southeastern Canada. It is usually found on floodplains or on sandy uplands and is usually seen growing in association with Quaking Aspen (*P. tremuloides*), from which it is easily distinguished by its large-toothed leaves. It provides an important habitat for nesting birds and other wildlife and the wood is also used for pulp.

WILLOW FAMILY, SALICACEAE

Deciduous
Up to 80ft

| J | F | M | A | M | J |
| J | A | S | O | N | D |

Swamp Cottonwood
Populus heterophylla

ID FACT FILE

CROWN
Narrow, open

BARK
Gray, smooth, darkening and becoming furrowed with age

TWIGS
Brown, whitish-hairy when young

LEAVES
Alternate, 4–7in, broadly oval, often heart-shaped at base, finely toothed, densely whitish-hairy when young, green above, paler and remaining hairy below, turning yellow in autumn

FLOWERS
Catkins up to 2½in, reddish-brown, pendulous, males and females on separate trees

FRUITS
Up to ⅜in, elliptical capsule, brown, splitting in 2 or 3 to release tiny cottony seeds

A relatively rare cottonwood, found along the edges of rivers and swamps, *Populus heterophylla* is a fast-growing colonizing species. It is found along the eastern coastal plain from Connecticut to Georgia, and also from northwest Florida to Louisiana, and north along the Mississippi delta as far as southern Michigan. Due to its rapid growth and colonizing habit, it is useful in maintaining swampland habitats but is otherwise not much used, neither by people or animals, although it is occasionally planted as a shade tree.

Deciduous
Up to 80ft

J	F	M	A	M	J
J	A	S	O	N	D

Quaking Aspen
Populus tremuloides

ID FACT FILE

CROWN
Narrowly rounded

BARK
Whitish-gray,
smooth,
darkening and
becoming
furrowed with
age

TWIGS
Reddish-brown,
smooth

LEAVES
Alternate, 3–4in,
broadly oval,
pointed at apex,
rounded at base,
finely toothed, on
very slender
stalks, green
above, paler
below, turning
golden in autumn

FLOWERS
Catkins up to
2½in, reddish-
brown,
pendulous,
males and
females on
separate trees

FRUITS
Up to ¼in,
elliptical capsule,
brown, splitting
in 2 to release
tiny cottony
seeds

The most widely distributed tree in the northern
hemisphere, Quaking Aspen is found across
Canada from Newfoundland to Alaska,
penetrating south along the Rocky Mountains
into New Mexico and Texas, where it is found
at elevations up to 10,000ft. In the east it is
found more or less east of a line from Minnesota
to Iowa. Like all aspens, it is fast-growing
and quick to colonize newly
disturbed sites. Quaking Aspen
also spreads by suckering from
the roots, often forming large
clonal colonies. An important
habitat tree, it is also planted
ornamentally and the wood
has a range of uses.

WILLOW FAMILY, SALICACEAE

Deciduous
Up to 30ft

J	F	M	A	M	J
J	A	S	O	N	D

Coastal Plain Willow

Salix caroliniana

ID FACT FILE

CROWN
Spreading

BARK
Gray, deeply
furrowed, scaly
and ridged

TWIGS
Reddish-brown,
hairy when young

LEAVES
Alternate,
1½–4in, narrowly
elliptical, finely-
toothed, hairy
when young, dull
green above, gray
or whitish below

FLOWERS
Usually
appearing before
the leaves, tiny,
in erect catkins
to 2in, yellowish,
males and
females on
separate trees

FRUITS
Up to ½in, pale
brown, pointed,
hairy capsule

A common willow of the southeast, found in a
variety of wetland habitats, alongside streams,
lakes and as part of swampland communities,
Coastal Plain Willow ranges from Pennsylvania,
south to Florida, and west to Texas.
Populations become more fragmented the
farther west along the Gulf Coast, and also
north to Nebraska. Its only use is in wetland
habit restoration, although many animals and
birds take advantage of the shelter it offers.

WILLOW FAMILY, SALICACEAE

Deciduous
Up to 80ft

J	F	M	A	M	J
J	A	S	O	N	D

White Willow
Salix alba

ID FACT FILE

CROWN
Open, spreading

BARK
Gray, furrowed,
and ridged

TWIGS
Brown, densely
hairy when young

LEAVES
Alternate, 2–4in,
lance-shaped,
finely toothed,
shiny green
above, densely
whitish-hairy
below

FLOWERS
Usually
appearing after
the leaves, tiny,
in erect catkins
to 2½in, hairy,
yellowish, males
and females on
separate trees

FRUITS
Up to ⅛in, pale
brown, narrow,
capsule

A common tree native to Europe and Asia,
but introduced to the United States in Colonial
days, White Willow is now naturalized in parts
of southern Canada and the eastern United
States. The wood is little utilized beyond as
fuel wood or for fencing, but the tree is widely
grown as a shelterbelt tree and also occasionally
planted as an ornamental.

WILLOW FAMILY, SALICACEAE

Deciduous
Up to 60ft

J	F	M	A	M	J
J	A	S	O	N	D

Peachleaf Willow
Salix amygdaloides

ID FACT FILE

CROWN
Irregular, spreading

BARK
Gray-brown, becoming scaly

TWIGS
Orange-brown, thin, flexible

LEAVES
Alternate, 2–4in, lance-shaped, narrowly pointed, finely toothed, shiny green above, densely whitish-hairy below

FLOWERS
Usually appearing before the leaves, tiny, in erect catkins to 3in, yellowish, males and females on separate trees

FRUITS
Up to ¼in, reddish-yellow, capsule

In the United States, this small tree is found from New York southwest to Texas, spreading northwest through the Rocky Mountains to Montana and Idaho; it is also found across southern Canada. Peachleaf Willow is a wetland species found alongside streams and rivers, often growing with cottonwood species. Although it has a widespread range across North America, it is generally locally uncommon.

WILLOW FAMILY, SALICACEAE

Deciduous
Up to 20ft

| J | F | M | A | M | J |
| J | A | S | O | N | D |

Pussy Willow
Salix discolor

ID FACT FILE

CROWN
Rounded

BARK
Gray, fissured
and scaly

TWIGS
Reddish-brown,
hairy when young

LEAVES
Alternate,
1½–4in, narrowly
elliptical,
sometimes
irregularly
toothed, hairy
when young,
shiny green
above, gray or
whitish below

FLOWERS
Usually
appearing before
the leaves, tiny,
in erect catkins
to 2in, with silky
white hairs,
males showy,
yellowish, males
and females on
separate trees

FRUITS
Up to ½in, pale
brown, narrow,
hairy capsule

Pussy Willow is a colonizing species of
wetlands, sometimes growing as a shrub, or
as a small, multistemmed tree. It is native
across southern Canada, and found in the
United States from Maine south to Delaware
and west to Missouri and Minnesota. Scattered
populations are also found in North Dakota
and Wyoming. An important habitat tree, it
is often grown ornamentally for the showy
flowers, and cut stems are harvested on a
commercial basis in early spring and forced
into flowering for the florist trade. The bark
and roots, in common with other willow
species, contain chemicals called "salicylates",
which are the basis for the drug aspirin.

WILLOW FAMILY, SALICACEAE

Deciduous
Up to 100ft

J	F	M	A	M	J
J	A	S	O	N	D

Black Willow
Salix nigra

ID FACT FILE

CROWN
Irregular,
spreading

BARK
Dark brown,
furrowed into
forking ridges

TWIGS
Orange-brown,
slender

LEAVES
Alternate, 3–5in,
narrowly lance-
shaped, long-
pointed, finely
toothed, dark
green above,
paler and often
hairy below,
turning yellow in
autumn

FLOWERS
Usually
appearing before
the leaves, tiny,
in erect catkins
to 3in, yellowish,
males and
females in
separate clusters
at ends of twigs

FRUITS
Up to ¼in,
reddish-brown
capsule,
hairless

A variable tree, but in parts of its range at least,
Black Willow is the largest of the North
American willows and the only one of
significant importance. The wood is used for a
variety of purposes and, because it roots so
easily from cuttings, this species is also very
useful in preventing soil erosion. The bark and
leaves were also formerly used for their
medicinal properties. Black Willow is found
from Maine south to Florida, and west to
Texas and Minnesota, although it also occurs
sporadically from western Texas to California.

HEATHER FAMILY, ERICACEAE

Evergreen
Up to 20ft

J	F	M	A	M	J
J	A	S	O	N	D

Texas Madrone
Arbutus xalapensis

ID FACT FILE

CROWN
Rounded

BARK
Gray or reddish-
brown, smooth,
peeling off in
large, thin plates
revealing lighter
bark beneath

TWIGS
Red, smooth,
hairy when
young, turning
reddish-brown

LEAVES
Alternate, 2–4in,
elliptical,
leathery, glossy,
dark green
above, paler and
hairy below

FLOWERS
Urn-shaped, ¼in,
white sometimes
tinged pink, in
terminal clusters
up to 6in

FRUITS
½in across,
globular, warty,
orange-red or
yellow

Texas Madrone is an uncommon tree that has a much wider distribution south of the United States in Mexico and Guatemala, but it is nevertheless well known in south-central Texas and west to eastern parts of New Mexico. It is found in dry, sunny canyons and on mountain slopes. Its smooth bark that is revealed beneath exfoliating old dark bark makes it an attractive ornamental tree. The wood is also used in the making of various utensils, and the leaves and fruits provide a valuable food source for local wildlife.

HEATHER FAMILY, ERICACEAE

Deciduous
Up to 50ft

J	F	M	A	M	J
J	A	S	O	N	D

Sourwood
Oxydendron arboreum

This species is a valued ornamental tree for its attractive foliage (which turns bright red in autumn) and pendent white flowers, which often occur together. It is naturally found from Pennsylvania and Maryland in the north, to Louisiana and Florida, and is also seen in the Appalachian Mountains. It is a constituent of upland pine and oak forests and has a distinct preference for moist, acidic soils. The flowers are very attractive to both butterflies and bees. A honey is also produced from the flowers.

ID FACT FILE

CROWN
Conical or rounded with ascending branches

BARK
Gray-brown, fissured into ridges

TWIGS
Green, slender, hairless

LEAVES
Alternate, 4–7in, narrowly elliptical, toothed, yellow-green above, paler and sometimes hairy below, turning red in autumn, sour tasting

FLOWERS
Small to ¼in, urn-shaped, white, in 1–sided, pendent clusters up to 10in at the ends of branches

FRUITS
½in, oval, brown, finely hairy, 5-celled, persistent

EBONY FAMILY, EBENACEAE

Deciduous
Up to 70ft

J	F	M	A	M	J
J	A	S	O	N	D

Common Persimmon
Diospyros virginiana

ID FACT FILE

CROWN
Pyramidal,
becoming open

BARK
Gray-brown,
fissured into
squarish plates

TWIGS
Reddish-brown,
often hairy

LEAVES
Alternate, oval,
2½–6in, pointed
at tip, shiny-
green above,
paler below,
turning yellow in
autumn

FLOWERS
Bell-shaped,
white, fragrant,
males up to ½in,
usually in 3's,
females up to
½in, solitary,
males and
females on
separate trees

FRUITS
Up to 1½in,
berrylike, red to
yellow, often
persistent

Extensively distributed throughout the
southeast, from Connecticut west to Iowa,
and south to Texas and Florida in a variety
of habitats, Persimmon is also quick to
colonize any new habitats. The somewhat
date-like fruit it produces is edible and has
been long used by people, and the wood
has good shockproof qualities. The fruit is
extremely unpalatable prior to the ripening
action of the first frosts; it ripens in
October–November. The fruits will usually
fall of their own accord once ripe. A slow-
growing species but one which is extremely
adaptable, hence its success in a variety
of habitats.

STYRAX FAMILY, STYRACACEAE

Deciduous
Up to 30ft

| J | F | M | A | M | J |
| J | A | S | O | N | D |

Carolina Silverbell
Halesia carolina

ID FACT FILE

CROWN
Open

BARK
Reddish-brown,
furrowed and
ridged

TWIGS
Brown, hairy
when young

LEAVES
Alternate,
elliptical, pointed
at apex, finely
toothed, dark
green above,
whitish-hairy
below, turning
yellow in autumn

FLOWERS
Bell-shaped,
small, up to ⅝in,
pink, males in
small clusters,
females solitary,
males and
females on
separate trees

FRUITS
Up to 2in,
elliptical with a
pointed tip,
reddish-brown,
with 4 wings

The Carolina Silverbell is native to the southern Appalachian Mountains in the southwest, from Virginia to Tennessee and Alabama where it is common. Localized populations are also found in Florida, Oklahoma, and Illinois. Of no commercial use beyond as a landscape specimen, it is nevertheless an attractive tree with pretty pink bell-shaped flowers emerging behind the new spring leaves.

ROSE FAMILY, ROSACEAE

Deciduous
Up to 30ft

| J | F | M | A | M | J |
| J | A | S | O | N | D |

Saskatoon Serviceberry
Amelanchier alnifolia

ID FACT FILE

CROWN
Spreading,
irregular

BARK
Gray-brown,
smooth,
becoming
fissured with age

TWIGS
Reddish, hairless

LEAVES
Alternate,
1¼–2½in, oval to
rounded,
toothed, dark
green above,
paler and
sometimes hairy
below

FLOWERS
Appearing with
the leaves in
erect terminal
clusters, 1¼in,
petals narrow,
white

FRUITS
¼in, purple,
apple-like, edible

Although predominantly a western species—
found from Alaska south along the Rockies and
Coastal Ranges to Colorado and California
respectively—*Amelanchier alnifolia* also ranges
as far east as Manitoba (and locally, eastern
Quebec) in Canada, and Minnesota in the
United States. It is a relatively common tree of
woodlands and clearings and the sweet fruits
are eaten by people and wildlife. Although the
species is not harvested commercially, its wood
is strong and sometimes exploited for a range
of uses, as are the young, willowlike branches.

ROSE FAMILY, ROSACEAE

Deciduous
Up to 20ft

J	F	M	A	M	J
J	A	S	O	N	D

Downy Serviceberry
Amelanchier arborea

ID FACT FILE

CROWN
Irregular

BARK
Gray, smooth, becoming fissured with age

TWIGS
Reddish when young

LEAVES
Alternate, 1½–4in, oval, toothed, softly hairy especially below, dull green above, paler below, turning yellow or red in autumn

FLOWERS
Appearing before the leaves in erect terminal clusters, 1¼in, petals narrow, white

FRUITS
⅜in, purple, apple-like, edible

A small tree found naturally as far south as Florida in the east, westward across to Oklahoma and Minnesota, but also widely grown as an ornamental due to its year-round interest. The common name refers to the downy white hairs on the new spring leaves, which protect the new growth. The tree produces attractive flowers and fruits (which are attractive to birdlife) and good autumn color.

ROSE FAMILY, ROSACEAE

Deciduous
Up to 30ft

| J | F | M | A | M | J |
| J | A | S | O | N | D |

Cockspur Hawthorn
Crataegus crus-galli

ID FACT FILE

CROWN
Broad, dense

BARK
Gray to brown, scaly

TWIGS
Stout, covered in long, slender, red-brown spines, up to 3in

LEAVES
Alternate, shiny, 1¼–4in, narrowly elliptical, narrower at base, toothed, leathery, dark green turning orange and scarlet in autumn

FLOWERS
½–⅜in across, white, with 2–3 styles, in clusters

FRUITS
½in, rounded, greenish to dull dark red, 2–3-seeded in drooping clusters

Easily recognizable with a wide spreading habit and clusters of white flowers in spring, this tree has been planted both ornamentally and as hedging since Colonial times. Naturally, it is often found as thicket-forming scrub at forest edges and is distributed throughout the eastern states as far south as Florida, west to Iowa and Texas. The long thorns which cover the branches and twigs have been used as pins.

ROSE FAMILY, ROSACEAE

Deciduous
Up to 30ft

| J | F | M | A | M | J |
| J | A | S | O | N | D |

Black Hawthorn
Crataegus douglasii

ID FACT FILE

CROWN
Broad, dense

BARK
Gray, scaly and
rough

TWIGS
Red, slender,
with curved
spines, up to
1¼in

LEAVES
Alternate, shiny,
1¼–4in, oval,
narrower at
base, toothed,
sometimes
lobed, dark
green, paler
below

FLOWERS
⅜–½in across,
white, with 3–5
styles, in broad
clusters

FRUITS
⅜–½in, rounded,
black, 3–5-
seeded in
drooping clusters

Black Hawthorn is a small tree with a tendency
to become shrubby in exposed areas. It has a
disjunct distribution, largely restricted to the
west coast, from Alaska to California arching
inland to Wyoming. Isolated populations are
also known from Minnesota and Michigan,
possibly due to previous human association. Its
main use is in soil stabilization; otherwise its
only real importance is its value to wildlife as a
food plant, although it is sometimes grown as
an ornamental tree.

ROSE FAMILY, ROSACEAE

Deciduous
Up to 20ft

J	F	M	A	M	J
J	A	S	O	N	D

Fanleaf Hawthorn
Crataegus flabellata

ID FACT FILE

CROWN
Irregular

BARK
Gray-brown, scaly

TWIGS
Brown, stout, with curved spines, up to 2½in

LEAVES
Alternate, shiny, 1–2in, elliptical, rounded at base, toothed, shallowly lobed, green above, paler below, turning yellow in autumn

FLOWERS
Up to ¾in across, white, with 3–5 styles, in dense clusters

FRUITS
½in, rounded, red, 3–5-seeded in drooping clusters, sometimes persistent

Fanleaf Hawthorn is a common tree known from Maine to Minnesota in the northeast, south to Louisiana and Georgia, although it is also often seen as a large shrub. It is a species of upland forests and meadows and a common component of montane habitats, especially in the Smoky Mountains, though it is less common farther south in the Appalachians.

ROSE FAMILY, ROSACEAE

Deciduous
Up to 60ft

J	F	M	A	M	J
J	A	S	O	N	D

Oneseed Hawthorn
Crataegus monogyna

ID FACT FILE

CROWN
Rounded, dense
to spreading

BARK
Gray to brown,
scaly

TWIGS
Slender, covered
in slender, red-
brown spines,
up to ⅜in

LEAVES
Alternate, shiny,
1–2in, ovate,
deeply 3–7-
lobed, dark green
above, paler
below

FLOWERS
⅜–⅝in across,
white or pink,
with a single
style, in flat
clusters

FRUITS
⅜–⅝in, rounded,
bright red with
a single seed

Often wrongly confused with English
Hawthorn (*C. oxyacantha*), this species, native
to, and long cultivated in Europe, reached
North America with the first pioneers. It is
now escaped and widely naturalized.
Sometimes grown ornamentally with various
single and double-flowered varieties in a range
of colors, it is also an extremely useful hedging
plant if kept cut.

ROSE FAMILY, ROSACEAE

Deciduous
Up to 30ft

J	F	M	A	M	J
J	A	S	O	N	D

Washington Hawthorn
Crataegus phaenopyrum

ID FACT FILE

CROWN
Dense, rounded

BARK
Pale brown, smooth when young, becoming scaly

TWIGS
Brown, with slender spines, up to 1½in

LEAVES
Alternate, shiny, 1–2in, broadly ovate but usually with 3 lobes and pointed at apex, toothed, green above, paler below, turning red in autumn

FLOWERS
Up to ⅜in across, pale yellow, with 3–5 styles, in dense clusters

FRUITS
Up to ¼in, rounded, red, 3–5-seeded in drooping clusters, persistent

Washington Hawthorn is so called due to being introduced from Washington, D.C. to Pennsylvania as long ago as the nineteenth century. Today, it is grown ornamentally all over the eastern states and has become naturalized as far north as southern Canada. Originally, its range would most likely have been from Missouri and Arkansas in the west, across to Florida and Virginia. It is no surprise that it is now so widely grown as it is one of the most attractive hawthorn species with pleasant foliage and autumn color, and sprays of pale yellow flowers in spring.

ROSE FAMILY, ROSACEAE

Deciduous
Up to 30ft

J	F	M	A	M	J
J	A	S	O	N	D

Southern Crabapple
Malus angustifolia

ID FACT FILE

CROWN
Open, broad

BARK
Gray-brown,
furrowed and
ridged

TWIGS
Brown, downy
when young

LEAVES
Alternate, 1–3in,
elliptical,
toothed, green,
above, paler
below, hairy
when young,
turning brown in
autumn

FLOWERS
1½in, in clusters,
5 petals, pink,
sepals, fragrant

FRUITS
¾–1in, fleshy,
greenish-yellow,
sour-tasting

Southern Crabapple is native to the southeast with a scattered but wide distribution. Its main range is from Virginia south to Florida and west to Louisiana and Arkansas although localized populations also occur in the northeast as far north as New Jersey. A small attractive tree, it is nevertheless liable to fungal disease in cultivation, although the dense wood is sometimes used for tool handles. In the wild it is an important food source for a wide variety of animals.

ROSE FAMILY, ROSACEAE

Deciduous
Up to 30ft

| J | F | M | A | M | J |
| J | A | S | O | N | D |

Sweet Crabapple
Malus coronaria

ID FACT FILE

CROWN
Open, spreading

BARK
Reddish-brown,
shallowly ridged

TWIGS
Gray, hairy, often
spurred

LEAVES
Alternate, 2–4in,
oval, coarsely
toothed,
sometimes lobed
at base, yellow-
green and
reddish-hairy
when young,
turning orange
and red in
autumn

FLOWERS
1½in, in clusters,
5 petals, pink,
opening white,
sepals, fragrant

FRUITS
1in, fleshy,
greenish-yellow

This species is the common crabapple of the northeast found in a variety of habitats, although preferring sunny, open situations such as meadows and forest edges and clearings. It ranges from New York and Georgia in the east, west to Mississippi, Arkansas, and Illinois. The fruit is important for wildlife and was also formerly used by people, drying the fruit or using it in preserves. The dense wood is used for tool handles and although an attractive ornamental tree, like other species of apple, it is susceptible to a range of fungal diseases.

ROSE FAMILY, ROSACEAE

Deciduous
Up to 50ft

| J | F | M | A | M | J |
| J | A | S | O | N | D |

Cultivated Apple
Malus pumila

ID FACT FILE

CROWN
Dense

BARK
Brown, fissured

TWIGS
Downy

LEAVES
Alternate,
1½–5in, elliptical,
toothed, dark
green, hairy
above, downy
below

FLOWERS
1in, in clusters,
petals 5, white
tinged with pink,
sepals, hairy,
persistent

FRUITS
2–4in, fleshy,
sweet-tasting

Of old hybrid origin, the Cultivated Apple was
introduced to the United States and widely
grown as an orchard tree for the copious edible
fruits it produces, used for a range of drinks
and foodstuffs. There are thousands of
cultivated forms and varieties and it can often
be found naturalized in areas previously
inhabited by human populations.

ROSE FAMILY, ROSACEAE

Deciduous
Up to 50ft

J	F	M	A	M	J
J	A	S	O	N	D

Wild Apple
Malus sylvestris

ID FACT FILE

CROWN
Dense

BARK
Gray, fissured
becoming scaly

TWIGS
Downy when
young, spiny

LEAVES
Alternate,
1¼–4½in,
elliptical,
toothed, dark
green, hairless

FLOWERS
¾–1¼in, in
clusters, petals
5, white,
sometimes
tinged with pink,
sepals, hairy,
persistent

FRUITS
¾–1¼in, hard,
sour

Now naturalized locally across the United States,
this is one of the parents of the Cultivated Apple
(*M. pumila*). Formerly cultivated in its own
right, the fruit is smaller and harder than that of
the Cultivated Apple, and is also sour-tasting.
Wild trees tend to be armed with spines and
have pure white flowers, whereas those in
cultivation tend to lose the spines and the
flowers are always tinged with pink.

ROSE FAMILY, ROSACEAE

Deciduous
Up to 30ft

J	F	M	A	M	J
J	A	S	O	N	D

American Plum
Prunus americana

A small attractive tree, this species is widely grown for its fruit, for which a number of improved cultivated varieties have been developed. It is also grown as an ornamental tree for the attractive clusters of white flowers. It is native from New Hampshire south to Florida and west to Oklahoma and Montana, south of the Great Lakes.

ID FACT FILE

CROWN
Irregular, broad

BARK
Dark brown, scaly

TWIGS
Pale brown, slender, hairless, ending in a spine

LEAVES
Alternate, 2½–4in, elliptical, pointed at tip, double-toothed, dark green above, paler below

FLOWERS
Appearing before the leaves, in clusters of usually 2–5, petals 5, rounded, white, to 1in

FRUITS
Up to 1in, red plum

ROSE FAMILY, ROSACEAE

Deciduous
Up to 20ft

J	F	M	A	M	J
J	A	S	O	N	D

Chickasaw Plum
Prunus angustifolia

ID FACT FILE

CROWN
Irregular,
spreading

BARK
Reddish-brown,
with horizontal
lenticels,
becoming
furrowed and
scaly

TWIGS
Reddish-brown,
occasionally
spined

LEAVES
Alternate, 1–3in,
lanceolate, shiny
green above,
paler below

FLOWERS
Appearing before
the leaves, in
clusters of up to
4, petals 5,
rounded, white,
to ½in

FRUITS
Up to ¾in, red or
yellow plum

Sometimes shrub-forming although also found as a small tree, Chickasaw Plum (also known as Sand Plum on account of its preference for sandy soils) has been cultivated since precolonial times, notably by the Chickasaw people, hence the common name. Thought to have originated in the central southern states of Texas and Oklahoma, it is now naturalized as far north as New Jersey and east to Florida. It is used for its fruits, which are often prepared as jellies or preserves.

ROSE FAMILY, ROSACEAE

Deciduous
Up to 30ft

| J | F | M | A | M | J |
| J | A | S | O | N | D |

Mahaleb Cherry
Prunus mahaleb

ID FACT FILE

CROWN
Open, spreading

BARK
Gray-brown,
fissured and
ridged

TWIGS
Brown, hairy
when young

LEAVES
Alternate, 1–2in,
elliptical, pointed
at tip, sharply
toothed, green
above, paler and
hairy below

FLOWERS
Appearing with
the leaves, in
clusters of up to
10, petals 5,
rounded, white,
to ⅜in, fragrant

FRUITS
Up to ½in, black
cherry

Native to western Asia, and eastern to
central Europe, and only introduced to the
United States, Mahaleb Cherry is grown
across both northwest and northeast
America. It has a vigorous rootstock and is
generally free of pests and diseases.
Consequently, it has been widely used as a
grafting tree for other species of cherry.
The seed kernels are edible and widely used
in food production in its native range. An
adaptable tree, Mahaleb Cherry can be
found in a wide variety of sites and
conditions, although it will generally not
tolerate sites that may become wet or which
have otherwise poor drainage.

ROSE FAMILY, ROSACEAE

Deciduous
Up to 13ft

J	F	M	A	M	J
J	A	S	O	N	D

Beach Plum
Prunus maritima

The Beach Plum is a somewhat shrubby, thicket-forming, small tree found along the Eastern Seaboard from Maine to Virginia. It is salt-tolerant and can also sometimes be found growing in cultivation, where it tends to be taller and less shrubby than in the wild where it grows in exposed sites. In its native dune habitat, it is important in erosion control and the edible fruits are also harvested for use in jams and preserves.

ID FACT FILE

CROWN
Broad, rounded

BARK
Reddish-brown, with horizontal lenticels

TWIGS
Reddish-brown, hairy when young

LEAVES
Alternate, 1½–2½in, elliptical, pointed at tip, finely toothed, green above, paler and hairy below

FLOWERS
Appearing with the leaves, in small clusters, petals 5, rounded, white, to ⅜in

FRUITS
Up to 1in, blue-black plum

ROSE FAMILY, ROSACEAE

Deciduous
Up to 30ft

J	F	M	A	M	J
J	A	S	O	N	D

Canada Plum
Prunus nigra

Canada Plum, as the name suggests, is native to the north, found from Maine south to Connecticut and west across to Illinois, Wisconsin, and Minnesota in the United States, and also in adjacent parts of Canada. It is not commonly cultivated, although several cultivated varieties have been developed, both ornamental and fruiting. The fruit is popular with wildlife and was also previously widely harvested and preserved by people.

ID FACT FILE

CROWN
Rounded

BARK
Gray-brown, darkening with age and becoming scaly

TWIGS
Brown, hairy when young, with spiny spurs

LEAVES
Alternate, 3–5in, elliptical, pointed at tip, coarsely toothed with gland at tip, green above, paler and hairy below

FLOWERS
Appearing with the leaves, in clusters of up to 4, petals 5, rounded, white, to 1in, fragrant

FRUITS
Up to 1¼in, red plum

ROSE FAMILY, ROSACEAE

Deciduous
Up to 30ft

| J | F | M | A | M | J |
| J | A | S | O | N | D |

Pin Cherry
Prunus pensylvanica

ID FACT FILE

CROWN
Narrowly rounded

BARK
Reddish-brown,
smooth,
becoming
fissured and
scaly

TWIGS
Reddish-brown

LEAVES
Alternate, 2–4in,
lance-shaped,
pointed at tip,
finely toothed,
green above,
paler below

FLOWERS
Appearing with
the leaves, in
clusters of up to
5, petals 5,
rounded, white,
to ⅜in

FRUITS
Up to ⅜in, red
cherry

Found across central and eastern Canada, Pin Cherry is found in the United States in a wide variety of habitats from Maine to Minnesota and south along the Appalachian Mountains to Georgia. It is a colonizing tree, especially after fire disturbance, and is also commonly found along hedges. It is not grown ornamentally and the wood is limited to use as a fuel wood. However, it is an important food source for local wildlife, and like Mahaleb Cherry (*P. mahaleb*) is used for grafting other cherries.

ROSE FAMILY, ROSACEAE

Deciduous
Up to 30ft

| J | F | M | A | M | J |
| J | A | S | O | N | D |

Peach
Prunus persica

This species, cultivated from ancient times, was introduced to the United States by Spanish colonists although it originally came from China. There are many cultivated varieties, both ornamental and fruiting, and it is now so widely grown that it has become naturalized in parts of western and eastern North America. It is, however, in common with other cultivated trees of the genus, subject to a range of pests and diseases.

ID FACT FILE

CROWN
Rounded, spreading

BARK
Gray-brown, smooth with horizontal lenticels, becoming scaly

TWIGS
Green, becoming reddish-brown

LEAVES
Alternate, 3–6in, lance-shaped, finely toothed, green above, paler below

FLOWERS
Appearing before the leaves, solitary but close together giving the appearance of clusters, petals 5, rounded, pink, to 1¼in

FRUITS
Up to 3¼in, yellow and red, rounded, hairy, peach

ROSE FAMILY, ROSACEAE

Deciduous
Up to 100ft

| J | F | M | A | M | J |
| J | A | S | O | N | D |

Black Cherry
Prunus serotina

ID FACT FILE

CROWN
Oval, spreading

BARK
Gray, smooth, becoming dark-gray and fissured

TWIGS
Reddish-brown, slender, hairless

LEAVES
Alternate, 2–6in, elliptical, tapering, finely toothed, shiny green above, paler and often hairy below

FLOWERS
Appearing after the leaves, in spikelike clusters up to 6in, petals 5, rounded, white, to ½in

FRUITS
Up to ½in, dark-red turning black, cherry

The most important of the native cherries to the United States, the Black Cherry has a variety of uses. It is widely distributed throughout the eastern states as far west as Texas in the south and Minnesota in the north. There are, however, several geographic varieties found as far west as New Mexico and Arizona. The timber, mostly harvested commercially in the eastern part of the range, is a fine-grained wood used in cabinet-making and furniture. The fruit is also harvested and the bark has medicinal properties.

ROSE FAMILY, ROSACEAE

Deciduous
Up to 20ft

J	F	M	A	M	J
J	A	S	O	N	D

Common Chokecherry
Prunus virginiana

ID FACT FILE

CROWN
Narrow

BARK
Gray-brown,
smooth,
becoming scaly

TWIGS
Reddish-brown

LEAVES
Alternate,
1½–3in, elliptical,
pointed at tip,
finely toothed,
shiny green
above, paler
below, turning
yellow in autumn

FLOWERS
Appearing with
the leaves, in
small clusters,
petals 5,
rounded, white,
to ⅜in, fragrant

FRUITS
Up to ½in, red or
black cherry

An extremely widespread species, Common
Chokecherry is found across the United States as
far south as southern California, northern Texas,
and North Carolina. It is also widely distributed
throughout southern Canada. It is generally a
colonizing species, which in turn becomes
replaced by more shade-tolerant species. It is
also grown ornamentally for the fragrant flowers,
and as a windbreak. The fruit was formerly
widely used in preserves and the leaves were also
used for medicinal properties.

ROSE FAMILY, ROSACEAE

Deciduous
Up to 30ft

J	F	M	A	M	J
J	A	S	O	N	D

American Mountain Ash
Sorbus americana

ID FACT FILE

CROWN
Open, spreading

BARK
Gray, with
horizontal
lenticels

TWIGS
Reddish-brown,
hairy when
young, with
prominent brown,
sticky buds

LEAVES
Alternate,
compound,
pinnate, leaflets
11–17, lance-
shaped, toothed,
up to 1in, pale
green, turning
yellow in autumn

FLOWERS
Tiny, white, in
flat-topped
clusters up to
5in, fragrant

FRUITS
Up to ¼in, apple-
like, red, in
dense clusters

In the wild, this adaptable tree is found on
moist soils in mixed hardwood forests from
swamps to rocky hillsides. Native to the
southeast of Canada, it is found as far south as
Georgia and Illinois although it tends to grow
in scattered populations in its southern range.
The bright red fruits are consumed by a large
variety of animals and birds. It is a very popular
ornamental tree and attractive both in flower
and fruit.

ROSE FAMILY, ROSACEAE

Deciduous
Up to 40ft

| J | F | M | A | M | J |
| J | A | S | O | N | D |

European Mountain Ash
Sorbus aucuparia

ID FACT FILE

CROWN
Open, spreading

BARK
Gray, smooth, sometimes becoming ridged with age

TWIGS
Brown, hairy when young

LEAVES
Alternate, compound, pinnate, leaflets paired (except at apex), 11–17, up to 2in, lanceolate, toothed, green, whitish-hairy below, turning red in autumn

FLOWERS
Up to ½in, cream, in dense flat clusters up to 6in

FRUITS
Less than ½in, berrylike, bright red, persistent

Native to wide areas of Europe, this species was most likely introduced to North America during Colonial times. Widely grown as an ornamental on account of the attractive bright red fruits (which are also extremely attractive to birdlife), the species has escaped from cultivation and is now naturalized across southern Canada to Alaska, and also across the northern United States. Often planted as a street tree, it naturally favors well-drained open sites and woodlands, often occurring in mountain sites giving the species its common name.

PEA FAMILY, FABACEAE

Deciduous
Up to 20ft

| J | F | M | A | M | J |
| J | A | S | O | N | D |

Sweet Acacia
Acacia farnesiana

Of unknown origin (although most likely
tropical North or South America), Huisache—
or Sweet Acacia as it is also known as today—is
widely cultivated both within and outside the
United States. Its native range may have
extended as far north as southern Texas but it
is today naturalized from Florida to southern
California. It forms a small spiny tree that
produces small, fragrant, yellow flowers,
produced in profusion in early spring.

ID FACT FILE

CROWN
Spreading

BARK
Gray, smooth,
darkening with
age

TWIGS
Brown, with
lenticels and
paired spines

LEAVES
Alternate,
compound,
bipinnate, up to
4in, 10–20
paired leaflets,
elliptical, gray-
green

FLOWERS
Up to ¼in, petals
yellow, in small
ball-like clusters,
fragrant

FRUITS
1½–3¼in,
cylindrical,
segmented pod,
brown, persistent

PEA FAMILY, FABACEAE

Deciduous
Up to 40ft

J	F	M	A	M	J
J	A	S	O	N	D

Eastern Redbud
Cercis canadensis

ID FACT FILE

CROWN
Spreading, somewhat rounded

BARK
Gray-brown, becoming furrowed

TWIGS
Brown, angled, hairless

LEAVES
Alternate, 2½–5in, heart-shaped, pointed at apex, petiole swollen, mid-green above, paler below, turning yellow in autumn

FLOWERS
Appearing before the leaves, pealike, up to ½in, petals pink, in clusters along branches and twigs

FRUITS
2½–3in, flattened pod, pink maturing dark brown, with flat, elliptical brown seeds within

This attractive ornamental tree is native to the central eastern states, from New Jersey to Nebraska in the north, and central Florida to Texas in the south. It is also widely planted in western North America for the bright pink flowers that emerge before the leaves, making this species especially striking. As with other members of the genus, the flowers are edible and the petals add sweetness to salads.

PEA FAMILY, FABACEAE

Deciduous
Up to 50ft

J	F	M	A	M	J
J	A	S	O	N	D

Yellowwood
Cladrastis lutea

An uncommon species found in scattered populations from southern Virginia and North Carolina in the east, west through Georgia to Oklahoma. It favors moist but well-drained limestone cliffs and ridges in mixed hardwood forests. However, it is increasingly planted as an ornamental tree for its year-round attractiveness and especially for the stunning summer floral display. The yellow heartwood is a source of a yellow dye. The dense wood is also a useful fuel-wood and is sometimes used for ornamental purposes as it is particularly attractive when polished.

ID FACT FILE

CROWN
Broadly spreading

BARK
Gray, smooth

TWIGS
Brown, slender, hairless

LEAVES
Alternate, compound, pinnate, leaflets 7–11 up to 4in, elliptical, shiny green above, paler below, turning yellow in autumn

FLOWERS
Up to 1¼in, pealike, white, fragrant, in pendent clusters up to 12in

FRUITS
2–3¼in, flattened pod, in clusters, inconspicuous

PEA FAMILY, FABACEAE

Deciduous
Up to 100ft

J	F	M	A	M	J
J	A	S	O	N	D

Honeylocust
Gleditsia triacanthos

This native of the Mississippi basin is a useful forage plant for animals, which eat the large fleshy fruits. Honeylocust is a very adaptable tree, able to cope with a wide variety of soil types and conditions. It is widely used as a street or ornamental tree. Some cultivated forms lack the characteristic abundant spines that cover the trunk and branches of the wild tree after 40–50 years.

ID FACT FILE

CROWN
Open, spreading

BARK
Brown, fissured into long ridges, with spines in branched clusters of 3 or more

TWIGS
Brown, stout, with long spines in 3s

LEAVES
Alternate, pinnate with many leaflets 1in, or bipinnate with many leaflets ½–1in, apex spined

FLOWERS
½in, bell-shaped with 5 greenish-white, hairy petals, in dense clusters, males and females in separate clusters or on separate trees

FRUITS
Up to 1¾in long, flattened pod, curved or twisted

PEA FAMILY, FABACEAE

Deciduous
Up to 70ft

J	F	M	A	M	J
J	A	S	O	N	D

Kentucky Coffee Tree
Gymnocladus dioicus

ID FACT FILE

CROWN
Narrow, open

BARK
Gray, thickly furrowed and peeling away on one edge

TWIGS
Brown, hairy when young

LEAVES
Alternate, bipinnate, leaflets 6–14, up to 3in, oval, green above, paler below, turning yellow in autumn

FLOWERS
Tiny, greenish-white, hairy, in erect clusters at the tips of the branches, males and females on separate trees

FRUITS
Up to 7in, leathery pod, reddish-brown, with rounded, shiny-brown seeds

This widespread but uncommon tree is found in scattered populations in a band running southwest from New York and Minnesota, to Oklahoma. The Kentucky Coffee Tree is found in a wide variety of habitats from limestone uplands to riverbanks but prefers moist soils. It has been introduced east of its natural range and is grown as a shade tree. The seeds, which are rumored to be toxic, were formerly roasted and used as a coffee substitute. The wood is used locally for cabinet making.

PEA FAMILY, FABACEAE

Deciduous
Up to 20ft

J	F	M	A	M	J
J	A	S	O	N	D

Honey Mesquite
Prosopis glandulosa

ID FACT FILE

CROWN
Open, spreading

BARK
Brown, thick, peeling in fibrous strips

TWIGS
Pale brown, with yellowish spines in pairs

LEAVES
Alternate, compound, bipinnate, usually with paired side-shoots, leaflets 10–16, up to 1¼in, oblong to lanceolate, green

FLOWERS
Tiny, yellow, in dense clusters up to 3in

FRUITS
Up to 8in, narrowly cylindrical pod, brown, with many edible beanlike seeds

The most widespread and most eastern of the mesquite species, *Prosopis glandulosa* is found naturally in Oklahoma and Texas, although it is possibly naturalized farther north. Its range also extends westward to Utah and southern California. The species has long been used as a food source and as a fuel wood and also for the high-quality honey—bees are attracted to the fragrant yellow flowers. Naturally found in sandy soils, the species is tolerant of drought and may also be found growing in desert grasslands.

PEA FAMILY, FABACEAE

Deciduous
Up to 80ft

J	F	M	A	M	J
J	A	S	O	N	D

Black Locust
Robinia pseudoacacia

ID FACT FILE

CROWN
Open

BARK
Gray, furrowed
into forking
ridges

TWIGS
Brown, with
paired spines at
nodes

LEAVES
Alternate,
pinnate, usually
7–19 leaflets in
pairs except at
tip, each 1–2in,
elliptical, bristle-
tipped, toothed,
blue-green
above, paler
below

FLOWERS
Pea-shaped,
white, fragrant,
in drooping
clusters to 8in

FRUITS
2–4in, flattened
pod, brown

Black Locust is naturally found in the
Appalachian Mountains from Pennsylvania south
to Alabama, and also in the Ozarks from Missouri
to Oklahoma, but also now widely naturalized
across the United States. It grows quickly and
also spreads by suckers; and older trees may
produce several trunks. The tree is widely grown
ornamentally and is also used for erosion control.
The durable wood is useful for fenceposts.

Evergreen
Up to 40ft

J	F	M	A	M	J
J	A	S	O	N	D

White Mangrove
Laguncularia racemosa

ID FACT FILE

CROWN
Rounded

BARK
Gray, smooth
with lenticels on
the lower trunk

TWIGS
Gray

LEAVES
Opposite, 2–3in,
oval, leathery,
shiny dark green,
with glands at
leaf base

FLOWERS
Up to ¾in,
greenish-white, in
erect clusters in
the axils of the
leaves, fragrant

FRUITS
Up to ¼in long,
pod, ribbed,
green, seed
germinating
inside pod

The smallest of the mangroves native to the United States, White Mangrove is often much smaller than other species, and also sometimes shrublike. It is native to the Florida coastline and Keys although also found in the Carribean and as far afield as tropical Africa. It is found at high-tide levels where it will tolerate occasional flooding, and where it produces peg roots, smaller and stouter than true pneumatophores, which stick up through the mud above high-water levels. As with Black Mangrove (*Avicennia germinans*), it also possesses salt glands on the leaves to help it survive the saline conditions. The bark is a source of tannins and the wood is exploited to some extent.

DOGWOOD FAMILY, CORNACEAE

Deciduous
Up to 30ft

J	F	M	A	M	J
J	A	S	O	N	D

Pagoda Dogwood
Cornus alternifolia

The Pagoda Dogwood is a major understory component of coniferous and mixed hardwood forests. It is an important food source for wildlife, the fruits being consumed by bears as well as birds, and the foliage being browsed by deer and other animals. The common name refers to the flat crown and tiered branches, which tend to droop under the weight of the blue fruits held on red stems, giving the appearance of a sloping pagoda roof.

ID FACT FILE

CROWN
Flat, spreading with horizontal branches

BARK
Reddish-brown, becoming fissured into plates

TWIGS
Greenish, slender

LEAVES
Alternate, 2½–4in, elliptical, minutely toothed, green above, paler and hairy below, turning red or yellow in autumn

FLOWERS
Up to ¼in, petals spreading, white, in flat terminal clusters up to 2in

FRUITS
Up to ¼in, berrylike, blue, in clusters on red stems

DOGWOOD FAMILY, CORNACEAE

Deciduous
Up to 50ft

J	F	M	A	M	J
J	A	S	O	N	D

Flowering Dogwood
Cornus florida

ID FACT FILE

CROWN
Spreading with
horizontal
branches

BARK
Reddish-brown,
fissured into
squarish plates

TWIGS
Greenish or
reddish, slender,
hairy when young

LEAVES
Opposite,
2½–6in, elliptical,
minutely toothed,
green above,
paler and hairy
below, turning
red in autumn

FLOWERS
Up to ¼in,
yellowish, in
dense clusters
up to ¾in,
surrounded by 4
large, white,
petal-like bracts

FRUITS
Up to ⅜in,
berrylike, red, in
clusters

An adaptable and widely utilized tree,
Flowering Dogwood occurs as a dominant
understory tree in deciduous woodlands from
Maine to Michigan in the north and Florida to
Texas in the south. It is an attractive tree in the
wild and also valued as an ornamental tree with
many cultivars now in existence. In addition,
the shock-resistant wood is exploited for a
variety of uses and the bark and roots were
previously harvested for medicinal and other
uses. It is also an important food source plant
for a variety of wildlife.

DOGWOOD FAMILY, CORNACEAE

Deciduous
Up to 100ft

J	F	M	A	M	J
J	A	S	O	N	D

Water Tupelo
Nyssa aquatica

ID FACT FILE

CROWN
Narrow, open

BARK
Gray-brown,
fissured into
scaly ridges

TWIGS
Reddish-brown,
hairy when young

LEAVES
Alternate, 5–8in,
oval, slightly
leathery,
toothed, shiny
green above,
paler and hairy
below

FLOWERS
Tiny, greenish,
males in clusters
up to ⅜in,
females solitary,
up to 10mm,
usually on
separate trees

FRUITS
1in, oblong,
berrylike, blue-
black, succulent,
sour

Water Tupelo, as its name suggests, is an
aquatic species found in swamps and
floodplains from Virginia to northern Florida,
west to Texas, and north along the Mississippi
river to Illinois. It developes a swollen,
buttressed base in order to cope with seasonal
flooding. It is of commercial importance as a
timber tree, producing good-quality timber
from the long, straight trunk, and is also known
as a honey tree.

DOGWOOD FAMILY, CORNACEAE

Deciduous
Up to 100ft

J	F	M	A	M	J
J	A	S	O	N	D

Blackgum
Nyssa sylvatica

ID FACT FILE

CROWN
Conical,
becoming flat

BARK
Gray, becoming
fissured into
large plates

TWIGS
Brown, slender,
sometimes
spurred

LEAVES
Alternate, 2–5in,
elliptical, slightly
leathery, shiny
green above,
paler and hairy
below, turning
scarlet in autumn

FLOWERS
Tiny, greenish,
males in clusters
up to ½in,
females up to
¼in in clusters,
usually on
separate trees

FRUITS
½in, oblong,
berrylike, blue-
black, succulent,
sour, usually in
pairs

Native to damp woodlands and swampy areas,
Black Tupelo is intolerant of drought. It is
found throughout the eastern states except in
the extreme northeast, as far west as Michigan
to Texas in the south, where a narrower-leaved
variety (var. *biflora*) is found. It is a handsome
tree with good autumn color and the fruit is
also much loved by small animals and birds.
A honey can also be made from the flowers
and the timber is also utilized.

HOLLY FAMILY, AQUIFOLIACEAE

Evergreen
Up to 30ft

| J | F | M | A | M | J |
| J | A | S | O | N | D |

Dahoon
Ilex cassine

ID FACT FILE

CROWN
Rounded

BARK
Gray, smooth, sometimes becoming warty

TWIGS
Brown, densely hairy

LEAVES
Alternate, oblong, leathery, 1½–3½in, shiny dark green above, paler below

FLOWERS
Tiny, white, in clusters with new leaves, males and females on separate trees

FRUITS
Up to ¼in, berrylike, red or sometimes orange or yellow, in small clusters, persistent

Dahoon is a holly of brackish, swampy areas and is native to North Carolina south to Florida, and west to Louisiana. It is a slow-growing, evergreen tree although it may tend toward being deciduous in the north of its range. It makes an attractive ornamental tree with its evergreen foliage; the red berries, which appear in winter, are used in Christmas decorations. The leaves were also formerly used as an infusion for tea.

HOLLY FAMILY, AQUIFOLIACEAE

Evergreen
Up to 70ft

| J | F | M | A | M | J |
| J | A | S | O | N | D |

American Holly
Ilex opaca

ID FACT FILE

CROWN
Narrow, dense

BARK
Gray, smooth,
sometimes warty

TWIGS
Brown, hairy
when young

LEAVES
Alternate,
elliptical,
leathery, 2–4in,
spiny-toothed,
dull-green above,
yellow-green
below

FLOWERS
Tiny, white, in
clusters with new
leaves, males
and females on
separate trees

FRUITS
Up to ¼in,
berrylike, red, in
small clusters,
persistent

A familiar tree with its spiny evergreen foliage and winter red berries, American Holly is found from Massachusetts south to Florida and as far west as Texas and Missouri. Commonly seen as an understory tree in a mixture of hardwood forests, it is an adaptable species. The pale wood can be dyed a variety of shades and is fine grained, used as inlay in cabinet making. It is also widely grown as an ornamental, and there are many hundreds of cultivated forms including those with yellow or orange berries, or variegated foliage.

HOLLY FAMILY, AQUIFOLIACEAE

Evergreen
Up to 20ft

| J | F | M | A | M | J |
| J | A | S | O | N | D |

Yaupon
Ilex vomitoria

ID FACT FILE

CROWN
Open

BARK
Reddish-brown,
scaly

TWIGS
Gray-brown, hairy
when young

LEAVES
Alternate,
elliptical, 1in,
toothed, shiny-
green above,
paler below

FLOWERS
Tiny, white, in
clusters with new
leaves, males
and females on
separate trees

FRUITS
Up to ¼in,
berrylike, red, in
small clusters,
persistent

Native to the coastal plain of the southeast, from
Virginia south to Florida and west to Texas and
Oklahoma, Yaupon is a small, spreading tree,
sometimes a shrub. It is found in a variety of
habitats from dry sandhills to swamplands, and
is salt-tolerant. It is sometimes grown as a
windbreak or trimmed hedge, and like other
hollies, for Christmas decoration. The young
leaves contain caffeine and can be used to
prepare a tea, which in high doses acts as an
emetic; the plant was previously used in this way
during ritual ceremonies. The fruits, which
persist into winter, are a good source of food
for wild birds and the tree itself being
evergreen also provides shelter.

HORSE-CHESTNUT FAMILY, HIPPOCASTANACEAE

Deciduous
Up to 100ft

| J | F | M | A | M | J |
| J | A | S | O | N | D |

Yellow Buckeye
Aesculus flava

A large tree found in rich damp woodlands from Pennsylvania south to Georgia in mixed woods, and also planted elsewhere ornamentally for its good autumn color. All parts of the tree are poisonous although in the past, the seeds were roasted and then leached to provide a nutritious food source. It is also a valuable timber tree.

ID FACT FILE

CROWN
Rounded

BARK
Gray, smooth, becoming gray-brown and peeling

TWIGS
Gray, smooth, with sticky winter buds

LEAVES
Opposite, palmate, 5–7 toothed leaflets up to 8in long, dark green above, yellow-green and hairy below, turning orange in autumn

FLOWERS
Appearing before the leaves, yellow, in terminal erect panicles up to 6in long

FRUITS
Up to 2½in, brown, husk spineless, containing brown seeds

HORSE-CHESTNUT FAMILY, HIPPOCASTANACEAE

Deciduous
Up to 70ft

J	F	M	A	M	J
J	A	S	O	N	D

Ohio Buckeye
Aesculus glabra

ID FACT FILE

CROWN
Rounded

BARK
Gray, scaly,
becoming
fissured

TWIGS
Reddish-brown,
with sticky buds

LEAVES
Opposite,
palmate, up to
6in long, with
5–7 elliptical
toothed leaflets,
yellow-green
above, paler and
hairy below,
turning orange
and yellow in
autumn

FLOWERS
Appearing before
the leaves,
yellow-green,
unpleasant
smelling, in erect
panicles up to
6in long

FRUITS
Up to 2in, brown,
husk spiny,
containing 1–5,
usually 3 brown
seeds

Native to the central part of the eastern United States, Ohio Buckeye is found from Pennsylvania to Alabama, and west to Oklahoma and Iowa in mixed hardwood forests. Now the state tree of Ohio, this species has a long history of human association— pioneers previously carried seeds with them to fend off rheumatism and the bark, despite being poisonous, was also used medicinally. The timber is used for furniture and the tree is also planted ornamentally for autumn color.

HORSE-CHESTNUT FAMILY, HIPPOCASTANACEAE

Deciduous
Up to 120ft

| J | F | M | A | M | J |
| J | A | S | O | N | D |

Horse Chestnut
Aesculus hippocastanum

ID FACT FILE

CROWN
Spreading, elliptical

BARK
Gray-brown, smooth, becoming fissured and scaly with age

TWIGS
Red-brown, smooth with large dark brown sticky winter buds

LEAVES
Opposite, palmate, 5–7 toothed leaflets up to 10in long, dark green above, paler below

FLOWERS
¾in across, 4–5 spreading petals, white spotted red and yellow at base with stamens protruding, held in erect branched panicles to 10in

FRUIT
Up to 2½in, green ripening brown, husk spiny, enclosing shiny brown seeds

This large tree is native to southeastern Europe but introduced across the United States, where it has escaped into the wild in the northeast. Planted as a shade and ornamental or street tree, it bears attractive panicles of white flowers in the spring. This species also produces the spiny fruits containing the seeds sometimes referred to as "conkers."

HORSE-CHESTNUT FAMILY, HIPPOCASTANACEAE

Deciduous
Up to 25ft

| J | F | M | A | M | J |
| J | A | S | O | N | D |

Red Buckeye
Aesculus pavia

ID FACT FILE

CROWN
Irregular, domed

BARK
Gray-brown, smooth

TWIGS
Reddish-brown

LEAVES
Opposite, palmate, usually 5 (–7) sharply toothed leaflets up to 6in long, dark glossy green above, dull green and often intensely white-hairy below

FLOWERS
2¼in long, bright red petals, in erect panicles up to 8in

FRUITS
Up to 2in, brown, husk spineless, containing shiny brown seeds

An understory tree of mixed forest along rivers and floodplains, this species is found from North Carolina to Florida, west to Texas, and north to Illinois. The showy red flowers and small size make this tree ideal for landscaping in parks and gardens. The crushed seeds and branches were used in the past to stun fish in local rivers and streams, and the bark is known to have medicinal properties.

MAPLE FAMILY, ACERACEAE

Deciduous
Up to 65ft

J	F	M	A	M	J
J	A	S	O	N	D

Box Elder
Acer negundo

ID FACT FILE

CROWN
Irregular

BARK
Gray-brown,
smooth,
becoming
fissured

TWIGS
Green developing
a gray-white
bloom in late
summer,
becoming
purplish, slender,
hairless

LEAVES
Opposite, 4–6in,
pinnate with 5–7
toothed,
sometimes lobed
leaflets, pale
green, mostly
hairless, turning
yellow in autumn

FLOWERS
Appearing before
leaves, males
with red anthers,
females greenish-
yellow and
insignificant on
different trees;
petals absent

FRUITS
Paired, brown,
winged, ¾in long,
persistent

This common, fast-growing, short-lived tree is
distributed throughout the Great Plains as far
south as Florida, with scattered populations
through to California. Uniquely amongst the
maples this species has pinnately compound as
opposed to palmately simple leaves making it
easily identifiable. Naturally found along
lakeshores and riverbanks, it readily colonizes
disturbed sites and a variegated form is often
grown ornamentally. Although the wood of this
species is of little commercial value, it is
sometimes exploited for simple boxes or
furniture, and a sugary drink can be obtained
from the sap.

MAPLE FAMILY, ACERACEAE

Deciduous
Up to 30ft

J	F	M	A	M	J
J	A	S	O	N	D

Striped Maple
Acer pensylvanicum

The Striped Maple is naturally found in the eastern states as far south as Georgia, and as far west as Minnesota as an understory tree in moist soils. It is also commonly seen as an ornamental on account of its distinctive, attractive striped bark, which gives the tree its common name. The bark and twigs are browsed by local wildlife as a winter food source.

ID FACT FILE

CROWN
Open, tapering

BARK
Green becoming gray with age, with vertical whitish stripes

TWIGS
Reddish when young, becoming green striped with whitish lines

LEAVES
Opposite, 4–7in, 3 lobes, toothed, pale green with hairs below when young, turning yellow in autumn

FLOWERS
Appearing with the leaves, yellow and insignificant, males and females usually occurring in separate clusters

FRUITS
Paired, greenish-brown, winged, 1¼in long

MAPLE FAMILY, ACERACEAE

Deciduous
Up to 65ft

J	F	M	A	M	J
J	A	S	O	N	D

Red Maple
Acer rubrum

A widespread eastern species found from Lake
Superior in the north as far south as the
Florida Everglades, it naturally prefers the
moist soils of marshes and riverbanks although
it will tolerate other nonalkaline soils. The
buds, young leaves, and flowers are all red in
color and the leaves ultimately turn a mixture
of bright yellow and scarlet in autumn.

ID FACT FILE

CROWN
Narrow or
rounded

BARK
Gray, smooth
when young,
becoming
fissured

TWIGS
Reddish

LEAVES
Opposite, 2–8in,
3 shallow lobes,
toothed, dull
green above,
whitish and hairy
below, turning
red and yellow in
autumn

FLOWERS
Reddish, in
crowded, short
clusters, males
and females
separate

FRUITS
Paired, red,
winged forming a
fork, ¾in long

MAPLE FAMILY, ACERACEAE

Deciduous
Up to 110ft

J	F	M	A	M	J
J	A	S	O	N	D

Silver Maple
Acer saccharinum

ID FACT FILE

CROWN
Open, irregular

BARK
Gray, smooth at first becoming furrowed and scaly

TWIGS
Greenish-brown

LEAVES
Opposite, 4–6in, 5 deep lobes, irregularly toothed, dull green above, silver-white hairy below, becoming pale yellow in autumn

FLOWERS
Reddish turning greenish-yellow, in crowded short clusters, males and females separate, petals absent

FRUITS
Paired, pale brown, winged, 2in long

A fast-growing tree naturally found throughout the eastern states as far south as Florida, east of a line from Minnesota to Oklahoma, although various forms are also widely grown as ornamentals. However, its native habitat of riverbanks and floodplains means the water-seeking roots can cause problems in an urban setting, as can the abundant fruit. The sweetish sap can be tapped and sugar obtained from the syrup but other species are more productive.

MAPLE FAMILY, ACERACEAE

Deciduous
Up to 100ft

| J | F | M | A | M | J |
| J | A | S | O | N | D |

Sugar Maple
Acer saccharum

ID FACT FILE

CROWN
Rounded, dense

BARK
Gray, becoming
rough and scaly

TWIGS
Greenish-brown
to gray

LEAVES
Opposite, 4–6in,
5 deep pointed
lobes with few
teeth, dark green
above, paler
below, turning
red, orange or
yellow in autumn

FLOWERS
Yellowish-green,
males and
females
occurring
together in
pendulous
clusters

FRUITS
Paired, red, or
yellow maturing
brown, winged,
1¼in long

An attractive tree often forming extensive stands throughout its range as far west as Minnesota to Kansas, and as far south as North Carolina, north to Maine and southeast Canada. Highly prized for its timber, which has a variety of uses, and also for its sap (the source of commercial maple syrup). The tree also produces intense autumn colors of red, orange, and yellow although its intolerance of pollution makes it unsuitable for urban sites.

CASHEW FAMILY, ANACARDIACEAE

Deciduous
Up to 20ft

J	F	M	A	M	J
J	A	S	O	N	D

Smooth Sumac
Rhus glabra

ID FACT FILE

CROWN
Irregular,
spreading

BARK
Gray-brown,
smooth,
becoming scaly
with age

TWIGS
Gray, smooth,
with whitish
bloom and small,
rounded, hairy
buds

LEAVES
Alternate,
compound,
pinnate, leaflets
11–31, leaflets
lanceolate,
2½–5in, toothed,
dark green
above, paler and
hairy below,
turning red in
autumn

FLOWERS
Tiny, yellow-
white, in dense
erect clusters up
to 8in, males
and females on
separate trees

FRUITS
Up to ⅛in,
rounded,
reddish, in dense
erect clusters

Smooth Sumac is the most widespread tree in the United States, native to all 48 contiguous states. The main center of distribution is in the east, although it is absent from the Mississippi delta and sporadic along the Gulf Coast. In the west it is largely restricted to montane habitats in the Rockies, where it grows at a higher altitude. It is typically thicket or colony forming and may also be shrublike. It is an attractive small tree with good autumn color, and there are several cultivated, ornamental forms.

CASHEW FAMILY, ANACARDIACEAE

Deciduous
Up to 33ft

| J | F | M | A | M | J |
| J | A | S | O | N | D |

Staghorn Sumac
Rhus typhina

ID FACT FILE

CROWN
Open, rounded

BARK
Gray-brown

TWIGS
Stout, forked, densely covered in velvety hair

LEAVES
Alternate, pinnate, usually 11–31 leaflets, each 2–5in, lance-shaped, toothed, dark green above, paler and hairy below, turning orange-red in autumn

FLOWERS
In dense conical clusters up to 8in at tips of twigs, males greenish, females red, on separate trees

FRUITS
Up to 2in, rounded, nutlike, red, hairy, in dense upright clusters, persistent

This small tree is restricted to the northeast of the United States and found no further south than South Carolina and Tennessee, and northwest to Minnesota. Staghorn Sumac is a thicket-forming species with downy, forking branches and will often develop more than one trunk through suckering. It is widely grown as an ornamental tree, largely on account of the vivid autumn foliage color.

CITRUS FAMILY, RUTACEAE

Deciduous
Up to 20ft

| J | F | M | A | M | J |
| J | A | S | O | N | D |

Hop Tree
Ptelea trifoliata

ID FACT FILE

CROWN
Narrowly rounded

BARK
Gray-brown,
scaly, aromatic

TWIGS
Brown, hairy

LEAVES
Alternate,
compound,
palmate, leaflets
3, elliptical, up
to 3in, hairy
when young,
unpleasantly
aromatic, green
above, paler
below, turning
yellow in autumn

FLOWERS
Up to ¼in, in
terminal clusters,
greenish-white

FRUITS
Up to 1in, disk-
shaped, with
papery wing,
ripening yellow-
brown, in
pendent clusters

Hop Tree has an extensive and wide
distribution, albeit scattered. It is found from
New York south to Florida and west to Texas,
from where it spreads north to the Great Lakes
area and Wisconsin. In addition, other isolated
populations are known in Arizona and Utah.
Probably as a result of such a scattered
distribution, there are many natural varieties
and forms and it also occurs as a shrub in places.
The common name relates to the fact that the
bitter fruits were previously used to brew beer.

VERBENA FAMILY, VERBENACEAE

Evergreen
Up to 40ft

| J | F | M | A | M | J |
| J | A | S | O | N | D |

Black Mangrove
Avicennia germinans

ID FACT FILE

CROWN
Rounded,
spreading

BARK
Dark gray,
smooth,
becoming thick
and fissured

TWIGS
Gray, hairy when
young

LEAVES
Opposite, 2–4in,
narrowly
elliptical,
leathery, shiny
dark green
above, whitish
and hairy below

FLOWERS
Up to ⅜in, white,
in dense,
terminal erect
clusters

FRUITS
Up to 1¼in long,
pod, pointed,
yellow-green,
hairy, seed
germinating
inside pod

Black Mangrove is found from Florida along
the Gulf Coast to Louisiana and Texas and also
occurs inland in sites that are exposed at low
tide. Of all the mangrove species present in the
United States, this is the hardiest and the one
that occurs farthest north. Like other water-
loving species, Black Mangrove produces
raised breathing roots called pneumatophores
to enable the tree to survive in its waterlogged
habitat. The leaves are also adapted to secrete
salt, helping the tree survive the saltwater of
the coast and brackish inland regions.

OLIVE FAMILY, OLEACEAE

Deciduous
Up to 27ft

J	F	M	A	M	J
J	A	S	O	N	D

American Fringetree
Chionanthus virginicus

This uncommon tree has a tendency to become shrublike, especially in cultivation. As a small tree it is particularly attractive, both in flower and in fruit. An understory tree of hardwood forests, it is found in moist soils in valleys and on ridges from New Jersey to Florida and west to Texas. The white flowers are fragrant and appear in large numbers followed by small blue fruits which are attractive to, and eaten by birds.

ID FACT FILE

CROWN
Open, spreading

BARK
Reddish-brown, somewhat scaly

TWIGS
Greenish, angled, hairy when young

LEAVES
Opposite, 4–8in, oblong, shiny green above, paler and often hairy below, turning yellow in autumn

FLOWERS
Up to 1in, with 4 linear, white petals, in 3's, in pendent clusters up to 8in, fragrant, males and females usually on separate trees, males with larger petals

FRUITS
Up to ¾in, elliptical, fleshy, dark blue

OLIVE FAMILY, OLEACEAE

Deciduous
Up to 100ft

| J | F | M | A | M | J |
| J | A | S | O | N | D |

White Ash
Fraxinus americana

ID FACT FILE

CROWN
Conical

BARK
Dark gray, intricately furrowed into a diamond pattern

TWIGS
Gray to brown, stout, usually hairless

LEAVES
Opposite, pinnate, leaflets 5–9, each 2½–5in, ovate, toothed, dark green above, whitish below and sometimes hairy, turning purple in autumn

FLOWERS
Appearing before the leaves, tiny, purplish, in clusters, males and females on separate trees

FRUITS
1–2in long, brown, winged, in pendent clusters

White Ash is a long-lived tree that is found along the slopes of valleys with other mixed hardwoods, its range extending from Canada as far south as northern Florida and as far west as Texas and Minnesota. White Ash is grown ornamentally for its typical purple autumn color, and the wood is much used in the manufacture of sports equipment.

OLIVE FAMILY, OLEACEAE

Deciduous
Up to 60ft

J	F	M	A	M	J
J	A	S	O	N	D

Black Ash
Fraxinus nigra

ID FACT FILE

CROWN
Narrow to rounded

BARK
Gray, corky, fissured into plates

TWIGS
Gray, ascending

LEAVES
Opposite, pinnate, leaflets 7–11, each 3–5in, lance-shaped, finely toothed, green above, paler and hairy below, turning brown in autumn

FLOWERS
Appearing before the leaves, tiny, purplish, in dense clusters, males and females on separate trees

FRUITS
¾–1½in long, pale brown, broadly winged, in pendent clusters

Black Ash is the ash found in the extreme northeast, from Minnesota and Iowa across to Virginia, and north into southeast Canada. It is commonly found in wet, peatland or bog areas. Occasionally, it struggles as a pioneer species in coniferous or deciduous woodland. It is named Black Ash for the dark heartwood it produces. This wood, however, is hardly used apart from being split into fibrous strips for baskets, barrel-hoops and similar products. Although of little or no commercial importance, this slow-growing species is an important habitat tree that provides refuge to small birds and animals, which also feed on the seeds.

OLIVE FAMILY, OLEACEAE

Deciduous
Up to 65ft

J	F	M	A	M	J
J	A	S	O	N	D

Green Ash

Fraxinus pennsylvanica

ID FACT FILE

CROWN
Densely rounded to irregular

BARK
Gray to reddish-brown, deeply furrowed

TWIGS
Gray, slender, usually hairless

LEAVES
Opposite, pinnate, leaflets 5–9, each 2½–5in, ovate, toothed, green above, paler below and hairy, turning yellow in autumn

FLOWERS
Appearing before the leaves, tiny, greenish, in clusters, males and females on separate trees

FRUITS
1¼–2½in long, brown, winged, in pendent clusters

The most widespread of the ashes in North America, the Green Ash is found throughout the eastern states and extending westward almost to the Rocky Mountains. It grows in a wide variety of habitats but has a preference for alluvial floodplains and is intolerant of shade. A resilient tree much used for shade and shelterbelts across the Plains, Green Ash is also a popular park tree.

FIGWORT FAMILY, SCROPHULARIACEAE

Deciduous
Up to 80ft

| J | F | M | A | M | J |
| J | A | S | O | N | D |

Princess Tree

Paulownia tomentosa

ID FACT FILE

CROWN
Broad, open,
with spreading
branches

BARK
Gray-brown,
shallowly
fissured

TWIGS
Brown, densely
hairy when young

LEAVES
Opposite, up to
18in, heart-
shaped,
sometimes 3-
lobed, with long,
pointed tip, pale
green and hairy
above, densely
gray-hairy below

FLOWERS
2½in long,
tubular, with 5
spreading,
unequal lobes,
violet, in erect
clusters 6–12in

FRUITS
Up to 2in, ovoid,
pointed at end,
glossy greenish-
brown

The Princess Tree is a native of China but has
been introduced as a widely grown ornamental;
it is now naturalized in many states where it is
found in open areas. The foxglove-like flowers
are conspicuous, appearing before the leaves
and are bright violet in color on the outside and
yellow inside. The flowers are actually formed in
the autumn of the previous year, remaining
dormant as hairy brown buds over winter.

BIGNONIA FAMILY, BIGNONIACEAE

Deciduous
Up to 65ft

J	F	M	A	M	J
J	A	S	O	N	D

Indian Bean Tree

Catalpa bignonioides

ID FACT FILE

CROWN
Broad, domed

BARK
Brownish-gray,
smooth
becoming scaly

TWIGS
Smooth, thick,
crooked, green
becoming brown

LEAVES
Opposite or in
whorls of 3,
ovate, pointed at
tip and heart-
shaped at base,
4–10in, dull
green above,
paler and hairy
below

FLOWERS
Showy, in erect
branched
clusters up to
10in, bell-
shaped, 5
fringed petals,
white, spotted
yellow and
purple, with 2
orange lines on
the inside, up to
2in across

FRUITS
Up to 12in long
and ½in wide,
beanlike pod,
pendulous,
brown

The Indian Bean Tree is native to southeast
North America—most likely originating from
the Alabama, Georgia, Mississippi, and Florida
area—but now is naturalized across the eastern
states as far north as New England and
west to Texas. Elsewhere it is
grown ornamentally. It has
become so widely established
because of its many attractive
features—large leaves, showy
flowers, and distinctive fruits.
It also makes an attractive
shade tree.

BIGNONIA FAMILY, BIGNONIACEAE

Deciduous
Up to 80ft

J	F	M	A	M	J
J	A	S	O	N	D

Northern Catalpa
Catalpa speciosa

Very similar to its southern relative *C. bignonioides*, Northern Catalpa is also of unknown definite origin, although the likely original range is thought to be the Indiana, Arkansas region. This species is now widely naturalized throughout eastern North America, and grown ornamentally elsewhere. It is slightly larger with larger flowers than its southern relative but otherwise virtually identical.

ID FACT FILE

CROWN
Broad, spreading

BARK
Brownish-gray, smooth becoming scaly

TWIGS
Smooth, thick, crooked, green becoming brown

LEAVES
Opposite or in whorls of 3, ovate, pointed at tip and heart-shaped at base, 6–12in, dull green above, paler and hairy below

FLOWERS
Showy, in erect branched clusters up to 8in, bell-shaped, 5 fringed petals, white, spotted yellow and purple, with 2 orange lines on the inside, up to 2½in across

FRUITS
Up to 16in long and ⅜in wide, beanlike pod, pendulous, brown, persisting on tree through winter

MADDER FAMILY, RUBIACEAE

Deciduous
Up to 20ft

J	F	M	A	M	J
J	A	S	O	N	D

Buttonbush
Cephalanthus occidentalis

ID FACT FILE

CROWN
Open, spreading

BARK
Gray-brown with vertical lenticels, becoming reddish-brown and fissured

TWIGS
Reddish-brown, hairless

LEAVES
Opposite or in whorls of 3, 2½–6in, elliptical, pointed at apex, shiny green above, paler below

FLOWERS
Tubular, up to ⅜in, petals white, style long and protruding, fragrant, in erect ball-like clusters

FRUITS
Up to 1in, globular, brown, with many 2-seeded nutlets

Buttonbush is a small tree native to the eastern states from Minnesota and Maine in the north to Texas and Florida in the south, with scattered populations also found in Arizona and California. This ungainly, much-branched species is generally shrublike in the northern part of its range, becoming tree-like in the south, where the foliage also becomes semi-evergreen. It favors wetland sites, where aquatic birds feed on the seeds. The foliage, however, is poisonous although the bark was previously purported to have medicinal properties.

PALM FAMILY, ARECACEAE

Evergreen
Up to 70ft

Cabbage Palmetto
Sabal palmetto

ID FACT FILE

CROWN
Rounded

BARK
Gray-brown

LEAVES
Alternate,
compound,
palmate, 3–6ft,
fan-shaped,
segments
pointed,
drooping, coarse,
green

FLOWERS
Tiny, white, in
large, branched,
drooping clusters
up to 3ft

FRUITS
Up to ½in,
berrylike, black,
in large branched
clusters

Cabbage Palmetto, or Cabbage Palm, is a fan palm native to sandy dunes and scrubland along the southeast coastline from North Carolina to Florida. It is found growing with a variety of species including pines and oaks, and has a distinct preference for moist to wet soils, and is even tolerant of occasional flooding. The trunks are sometimes used for pilings, and the edible leaf buds were also formerly harvested. Nowadays it is mostly exploited on a sustainable basis for the leaf fibers, or grown as an ornamental street tree in the southeast.

INDEX

PICTURE CREDITS